P9-DVD-356

The Emotion Handbook:

For the Recovery and Management of Feelings

by
Valerie Kack-Brice,
MSW, LCSW, BCD
Clinical Social Worker

Edited and Cover Design
by James Van Treese

*Best Wishes & Blessings
Valerie Kack-Brice
7-27-92*

Northwest Publishing Inc.
5949 South 350 West
Salt Lake City, UT 84107
801-266-5900

Copyright © Valerie Kack-Brice
1992
Northwest Publishing Inc.
5949 South 350 West
Salt Lake City, Utah 84107
801-266-5900

International Copyright Secured

Reproductions in any manner, in whole or in part,
in English or in other languages, is prohibited.
All rights reserved.

ISBN #1-880416-18-2

Printed In the United States of America

For Patrick

With gratitude for all the hours I borrowed
from your childhood, may this gift strengthen
you in your adulthood.

For Don

With appreciation for tolerating my
extravagance and supporting my dreams.

In memory of
Walter Pointon,
a model of dedication, determination and optimism.

ACKNOWLEDGMENTS

With appreciation I thank all my clients who, over the years, have been the true teachers. I am honored to have known them.

Those closest to me have given much support and encouragement. Thanks to my husband, Don Brice, for his love, first run critiques, and for the year to write. My son Patrick's occasional back rubs and hair brushing helped me stay connected during the many hours while I typed away. Don Brice Sr. generously provided the PC, encouragement to push through the technological intimidation, and got me out of more than one command jam. With trepidation and relief I gratefully received comments on the manuscript by my two precious mothers and sister Sherry.

For invaluable insight and honest editing, I thank June Schwartz, D Hansen, and Dr. Susan Mehra. For unfailing belief in me, uncompromised loyalty and encouragement in all matters of the heart, I bow to Ann Todd Jealous. For listening to my complaints and forgiving my inattention, I am grateful to Cheryl Allen. For years of impeccable teamwork and deepening my understanding, I thank Linda Parenzan Grotke.

I wish to acknowledge Dr. Linda Bailey-Martiniere and Bronwyn Jones for their timely encouragement and for reading the manuscript. Thanks also to James Van Treese at Northwest Publishing for recognizing this work and making it available.

For all those wonderful writers, teachers, and models from whom I have gleaned much of the fundamental wisdom for this book, I regret the lack of specific reference and ask forgiveness for anything of theirs I have gratefully claimed as my own. Finally, thanks to Pia Mellody, mentor, model and angel of mercy, for helping me discover my dignity and joy, and for the tools to share them.

VKB

PREFACE

The material for this book arose out of many years of hearing similar stories from clients. They complain: "I am either out of control or numb." Generally, once the crisis is resolved, or the historical catharsis is reached, people find that living in their emotions is chaotic or unmanageable. Observation has revealed to me that many people lack models for and information about appropriate emotional behavior. The most common request I hear is "tell me what to do when I am upset."

My parents were raised during the depression. Survival meant "pull yourself together, work hard, and don't feel too much." As a consequence, their parenting lacked understanding, experience and guidance around embodying and expressing pain, shame, anger and fear. They knew how to rage and lust, however. Unfortunately, this combination produced overachieving offspring who knew very little about self-care, lacked confidence, tended toward depression or hostility, and had little ability to create intimate, long-lasting relationships. Many people experience some form of emotional censoring such as this.

There is an expectation in this culture that we will "figure out" how to take care of ourselves and connect with others. What is more true is that we are ill-prepared, naive, and generally unable to be whole human beings. As adults we practice a lot of behavior toward ourselves that is unloving and destructive, such as overworking, indulging in drugs, alcohol, and food, or isolating. Eventually, we wind up parenting another generation and find that we have no idea how to nurture, attend to and provide respectful structure for these children. Then we despair over "what is wrong with them." The cycle continues.

This book is meant to be a map with many routes to appropriate emotional behavior. The first goal is to provide a language for talking about feelings. Since many people grow out of families where certain emotions are "allowable" and others aren't, I wanted to give people a way of recognizing a previously unidentifiable feeling by locating the place in the body where it is generally felt. Secondly, there is increasing evidence that unexpressed (repressed, suppressed or denied) feelings eventually erode the body's ability to remain physically vital. Disease, pain and poor functioning can result from a person's mismanagement of particular emotions. This often entails disregarding the body's natural inclination to protect itself, cry, flee, smile, or blush. Some suggestions are made for physical problems that potentially result from this pushing away of certain emotions. Since many people have quite skewed ideas of functional emotional expression, the third goal is to provide several options for expressing a feeling. Many of our models behaved extremely—either raging or stony silence, suicide attempts or medicating pain with alcohol or prescription drugs, etc. I offer guidelines for healthy self expression, both personally and on a community or global level. Lastly, because they work so successfully to change negative thinking, I encourage the practice of affirmations.

Underlying the suggestions for healthy emotional living is a belief that wholeness is achieved by balancing the many aspects of being human. This entails acting moderately in all physical, spiritual, intellectual, economic, and sexual activity. Emotional aliveness can be had without intensity and extremes. This guidebook offers a life-style that can be nourishing, passionate and fulfilling.

Originally, the book was conceived for my clients who were repeatedly asking for specific direction for handling their anger, pain, fear or shame. As they got well, they then asked for help in having their joy! I also had in mind other professionals who were dealing with these same questions from their clients. Resistance aside, most people are eager for alternative behavior that will allow them to get closer to the people they love, feel better about themselves and avoid serious illnesses. I was also focused on those clients who had done their cathartic grieving for their lost childhood, their lack of nurturing, or their emotional wounds left by abusive and neglectful parents. They continued to need guidance on day to day living.

The generation of these ideas came also from a conviction that the planet will survive the ravages that threaten her only if human beings act responsibly and thoroughly to find balance in themselves. We cannot expect to feel compassion for the plants, animals, and indigenous people who inhabit a mineral rich environment if we cannot feel our own pain, fear and shame. My hope is that with greater access to a healthy emotional conscience, humans will make decisions based on caring, compassion, concern for the future, and a sense of guardianship, rather than greed, oppression, and non-renewable resources.

As the book unfolded, it became increasingly evident that most people would benefit from practicing the suggestions offered and so, I wrote it for anyone seeking support for and guidance around living in a complicated and emotionally taxing world. Lastly, I wrote it for the parents, grandparents, aunts and uncles, friends and teachers of children. These guidelines are what we all should have been given from knowledgeable, mature, and safe people. Perhaps even a handful of children will know emotional wholeness from this offering.

VKB

TABLE OF CONTENTS

PART I

ASSUMPTIONS AND GUIDELINES

Chapter 1

WHY A HANDBOOK?

Many of us emerge from our childhoods not knowing how to manage our emotional lives. We feel either terrified or fearless, enraged or silent, arrogant or worthless, bored or ecstatic—in some extreme that is usually problematic to ourselves or to those around us. Further, we often have little or no access to our emotional lives—that part of ourselves that distinguishes us from much of the animal kingdom. No wonder we act with so little regard to ourselves or others, or that we spend so much time in states of depression, numbness, or aggression. We have lost our humanity.

Our task as adults is to "act like" adults (and I guess that means moderately and reasonably). The problem most of us face, however, is how to do this without ever having been given instructions, appropriate modeling, permission to explore new feelings or behaviors, or the safety associated with someone who might guide, nurture and support the process.

The most common complaint I have heard as a psychotherapist has been in the area of emotions: "She complains that I don't share my feelings and when I do, she says that I am not doing it right;" "You ask me to allow myself my anger or pain, but I don't know what you mean or how to do that."

Those of us from less than nurturing families often have suppressed, repressed, denied, or are so extreme in our emotions that we often have little access to or know how to express our true undefended feelings. Personally and as a therapist, I have had to be creative in discovering ways of accessing and expressing new-found emotions. I have asked others what they do and how they learned to do it and have gleaned much good advice. I also found excellent therapists who helped open the floodgates and taught me how to manage the emotions that came through. My goal here is to offer a course to the identification and expression of our true emotional lives.

As a psychotherapist, I have found that people want a snap solution to their emotional distress. Pain hurts, fear is uncomfortable, shame is hardly tolerable, and rage usually brings worse consequences. We want to get to equilibrium as quickly as possible. Once we get some relief from the chaos inside, we can focus and analyze, assimilate and digest, plan and refine new strategies.

This quick reference guide is intended for use in recognizing one's emotions and for practicing appropriate emotional behavior. The first part of the book includes chapters on the basic assumptions I make about human beings, guidelines for practicing the various emotions and emotional behaviors, getting distance when we need to be calm, and working with the inner child-self. Chapters follow on ten basic feeling categories that include a definition of each emotion and its variations, where in the body it is experienced, what happens physically and behaviorally when the emotion is denied or repressed, behaviors to aid in experiencing and expressing each emotion, and affirmations that will speed the process and retrain automatic responses.

Poor parenting results in specific adaptations called defense mechanisms. While, in childhood these "defenses" serve us well, we may find in adulthood that these adaptations no longer serve us and often work to our detriment. We have become disengaged from our true selves and must endure the

distress of discovering and exploring those aspects of ourselves that have been lost to us—mainly our emotions. The
journey to emotional wholeness is often a grief process and as
we know from the work of Elizabeth Kubler-Ross, grief can
take us through several different emotions. Many times,
emotions arise from childhood memories that emerge as we
seek understanding of our current life problems or as we open
ourselves to looking at the truth of what our experience was
as children. This can and often must be facilitated by a trained
therapist. As the reality of our uncovered history settles within
us, we begin the long journey of finding new ways to be in the
world.*

This handbook will serve as a support and resource when
recovery gets difficult, a guide and model for appropriate
emotional behavior, and a challenge to reach beyond the
familiar. This information is intended as a reminder that we
are faced with the task of recovering and tempering our own
humanity if we are to survive as a species. We also must learn
to accept and honor the humanity of others.

* Recognizing childhood wounds can be very difficult
since one of the most effective ways we survive is by denying
and repressing painful memories. Children need to believe
their parents love them and will tend to protect them by
warding off any possibility that harm was done. If you suffer
from any of the symptoms mentioned, there is a chance you
have some wounds that need attention. Please consult resources
such as *Facing Codependence*, by Pia Mellody, or any of
Alice Miller's books to discern a clearer picture.

FURTHER READING

1. Kubler-Ross, Elizabeth. *On Death and Dying* * A thorough and clear guide to understanding grief; it is useful to any grieving process.

2. Mellody, Pia. *Facing Codependence*, San Francisco, Ca.: Harper Row, 1989. This is the most elegant and useful model for understanding codependence, family dysfunction and adult symptoms available. Read it.

3. Miller, Alice. *Drama of the Gifted Child* * An extremely necessary look at parenting and how we come to be.

4. Talbot, Michael, *The Holographic Universe*. NY: Harper Collins Publishers, 1991. Sites much of the research supporting many of the ideas in this book. Aside from that, I highly recommend reading this fascinating view of how the universe is organized.

Chapter 2

TWELVE BASIC ASSUMPTIONS ABOUT HUMAN EMOTIONS AND CHANGE

Having suffered for years as a child from an alcoholic family and later having sought for spiritual understanding, I have learned some ways of managing my life that have been enormously helpful. From these experiences I make some basic assumptions about human emotions and change.

1. Human beings are perfectly designed to feel. We are given tear ducts and blood vessels in our faces for weeping and blushing. We have automatic responses in our large muscles for fleeing and fists for fighting. We use our voices loudly for defending or softly for nurturing. We have adrenaline that pulses through our bodies to enable us to do untold feats to protect or defend. Muscles in our faces contract to give us smiles or laughter. We have estrogen and testosterone that compel us to lust or have sexual intercourse. Our bodies are our profoundly complex and miraculous universe in which we house our emotional lives.

2. We have purpose. We were not made with such intricate detail and perfect harmony of related functions on a whim. The miracle of our physical form was purposeful and so brilliantly conceived and executed that humans are just now beginning to understand themselves. Emotional vitality is intrinsic to our being. Management of our emotions, therefore, our humanity, will bring us back from the brink of global

destruction and deliver us to the highest level of human evolution imaginable. If we can feel pain about oppression, poverty, environmental devastation, and violence, we surely will act more responsibly to end these atrocities.

3. Our emotional life is greatly affected by our physical and environmental well-being and our emotions in turn effect the condition of our physical and environmental vitality. We are a part of a perfect harmony of functioning and as we act responsibly toward our bodies we create more balanced energy and have a greater sense of well-being. Eating well, getting adequate sleep, frequent exercising, having quiet reflective time and contemplating higher spiritual teachings are essential ingredients to personal equilibrium. Applying the idea of "walking gently upon the earth" adds a dimension of planetary self-care by recycling, conserving energy and supplies, sharing resources, having community consciousness, preserving ecology, etc. Feeling more balanced physically and environmentally, we will find our emotions to be more balanced. Because we experience fewer extremes emotionally, we will be better able to take care of ourselves and act with consciousness in our environment.

4. Understanding our history is essential to understanding our emotions. Knowing that a parent was unreliable or unpredictably mean during our toddler years helps us to understand the root of a phobic response to heights or public places. Knowing that we rage at our spouses or children because we observed in our own parents enraged behavior or controlling silence may deter us the next time. Understanding that our controlling or caretaking behavior is like what our parents modeled as love is helpful. Understanding is the prerequisite to change. Pia Mellody calls this "getting your history straight." (1) She urges us to confront the "skewed thinking" by labeling behavior accurately. She gives us a long list of various ways in which we get wounded as children. The

wounding leads to unmanageable feelings and eventually to unhealthy and dysfunctional behavior. Once we understand the roots of our emotional or behavioral extremes, we open ourselves to understanding appropriate and functional emotional responses

Our emotional life is largely dependent on our thinking and understanding. We have the ability to choose new behaviors or to moderate our emotions by attending to our thinking. Using the intellect to "reframe" an event, we have the option to view things in a different light, context or intention. (2) Seeing that the water pipes froze and burst, we may choose to rant and rave about the inconvenience or we can see it as an opportunity to take care of some needed winterizing we had put off doing. Essential to our ability to change our behavior, we need tools and experiences that will help us see that we are in charge—we are not being victimized by the world outside, it is all within our reach to change.

5. Changing our behavior will often bring about a change in our emotions. The most obvious example of this is what occurs when we stop addictive behaviors. Our behavior may become more extreme at first, but then we gradually begin to gain a sense of comfort and balance in our responses to situations and other people. Sometimes in my practice I will recommend that a client target a particular behavior to change and I will devise with him/her a plan to accomplish this. This may be a behavior that usually gets a negative response from others or a behavior used frequently to keep certain feelings from arising. Often it will be a behavior that leads one further away from feeling whole and productive.

When Liz and Mark argued they each responded differently to the tension. Liz found any disagreements frightening and would demand that Mark stay and talk with her. Unconsciously, she was convinced that Mark would leave if he was angry with her. Liz's experience as a child was that when her parents argued, her father would leave and get drunk and her mother would retreat to her bed with a "migraine." As a child, Mark's father would stand over and rage at him insisting that Mark look at him. As a result, Mark felt frightened and engulfed by Liz's anger and needed time to figure out what he felt and thought when they argued. His response to a confrontation was to "get space" by leaving the room for a few minutes. Both Liz and Mark wanted to stay connected and each tried to do this, she by clinging and he by retreating briefly. Their behaviors repeatedly pushed their partner into a panic and then a defensive rage to ward off their fears.

As we worked in therapy, Liz and Mark discovered new ways to support each other during arguments. Liz asked Mark to let her know during an argument why he was leaving and when he would return. He asked Liz to lower her voice and stand further away from him when she was upset. Eventually, by practicing these and some specific communication skills, they were able to articulate their fears and ask for assurance from each other while they were disagreeing.

6. Being committed and focused in our quest for healing is necessary for our emotional recovery. I have known no one who has healed the wounds of childhood without having intensely uncomfortable periods of deep pain, fear, shame or rage. We are not given models for, nor are we asked to exercise much self discipline in our alcoholic or chaotic families. Many of us grow up thinking that "discipline" is a dirty word, or at best, that it is what our parents called beating us. However, any time we have set a goal and followed through on it, especially when it has required following a specific routine over and over, we experienced self-discipline. Brushing our teeth every day may have been what led to a good report from the dentist. We all know what a relief it is not to have the dentist drill holes in our teeth. Commitment, practice and determination are necessary to finding emotional well-being.

7. Emotions are experienced as waves of energy that move throughout the body as a wave moves toward the shore. They generate from our center (solar plexus?) and build, as a wave will swell, crest and then subside. And again, the wave will rise, spill over, and abate. With each cresting, the intensity will diminish. If we build a dike against the pounding of the wave on the shore, a wall against the spilling over of the emotion, that emotional wave will gather power, intensity or pervasiveness and will eventually erode and undermine until it can no longer be contained. We will get physically ill or isolated or we may attack with rage. Far more damage occurs when we go against the natural ebbing and flowing of our feelings. We build our dikes of fear, procrastination, avoidance, somatizing, addictions, etc.

We fear most that we will lose control, become crazy, die or hurt someone if we tap into the reservoir of repressed or denied emotions. Feeling overwhelmed is more about the experience of the child than it is about the reality of the adult. Remember, we are perfectly designed to have our feelings. We are ill equipped as children, however, to be overwhelmed by our parents' denied or out of control feelings and so we develop defenses against being overwhelmed. (3) When we understand this, give voice to the child in us and give back to our parents their emotions (through a specific therapeutic process), we begin to experience the lightness and manageability of our own emotions.*

8. One emotion will often mask another. I grew up thinking that screaming at someone or silent withdrawal was the way to let another person know I was hurt by what they said or did. The expression of pain was not in my emotional

---

* John Bradshaw, in his book *Homecoming*, offers some methods for doing this work.

repertoire. When I was suicidal as an adolescent, no one in my family recognized that I was in trouble, nor could they offer any support. When I did ask for help, I was told to "go to bed and stop worrying." Several years of sorting through the rage helped to find the original hurt. Permission from friends gave brief moments of tears. Finally, deep grief work with a therapist was necessary for me to be able to recognize fully my pain, ask for help with it, and receive the help I was given. Now when I raise my voice or feel like withdrawing I can recognize that I am hurting and needing some comforting or reassurance. Getting to know, feel and understand behaviors associated with our various emotions will help us reduce confusion and frustration when it comes to communicating them. This may be as simple a task as learning to identify what you already experience in your body.

I worked with a man whose wife complained that he "didn't have any emotions and wouldn't talk (to her) about them if he had any." In telling his history, David reported that he grew up in a very loving family. His parents were fairly available with their time and attention, there were lots of family activities and guidance was given when it was requested. I was puzzled by his difficulty in sharing feelings. As we worked together, I made several observations: that David was able to cry easily when he was hurt, he could confront other men in his therapy group when he as annoyed, and he reportedly gathered elaborate safety techniques for his backpacking and skiing hobbies to assuage his fear. I recognized that he had a very full emotional life for he expressed pain, anger and fear. In his family of origin, he simply had not received the language necessary to identify what he was feeling and so he was unable to "talk" about his feelings. His wife perceived his lack of "shared feelings" as an inability to feel. His therapy consisted of modeling from other men and labeling his various experiences with emotional language. As one gets adept at discriminating between the subtle variations of emotional categories, one can begin to talk about and express more directly what one feels.

9. In the retrieval of our emotional life, we may have to go to extremes. Sometimes, we will go to opposite extremes. Instead of not spending any money on ourselves, we may have to go "hog-wild" on a few shopping sprees as we give ourselves permission to experience the joy of self nurturing. Soon, we must learn moderate joyfulness in the area of spending, however, or go broke. As one continues to be conscious of ones emotions, finding appropriate ways to express them, moderation will begin to pervade. Be assured that I am not advocating dullness as a way of being in the world. Moderate emotional behavior is NOT dull, boring or controlled. The 12 step programs refer to moderation when they talk about serenity. When we have moderation, we feel centered (balanced?), empowered, and have a sense of well-being. This is what adulthood feels like.

10. There are ten basic categories of emotions with which we struggle the most: love, joy, pain, spiritual pain, anger, fear, shame/guilt, loneliness, lust and forgiveness. Each category can contain countless subtle variations. (Some of these variations are listed at the beginning of each chapter.) Using a common feeling language to describe our internal experience communicates trust, vulnerability, sensitivity, and bridges the chasm left by distrust, defensiveness, and aggression.

11. When we are familiar with these feelings, we can recognize that each is associated with particular physical areas in our bodies. It then follows that when we deny or repress a particular emotion, there will be physical repercussions. Disease sets in and creates circumstances which demand that we at least address the physical feelings. We also can effect our physical state through emotional work. (5) There are many studies that support this theory that our psychology affects our

physical well being. Dr. Bernie S. Siegel sites several examples in *Love, Medicine, & Miracles*. In the sections on each emotion, I have identified possible trouble spots in the body.

This is by no means meant to be a diagnostic tool to replace medical care, but rather a guideline for assessing the possibility of imbalance in the emotional arena. These suggestions arise from my own observations and some readings that will be noted. At the very least, physical problems are an indication that there is a need for greater or more specific self care.

12. Sometimes a particular emotional state becomes chronic, such as can occur with depression. This happens for many different reasons, not the least of which may be a chemical imbalance or allergy. I always refer clients with seemingly pervasive and difficult to treat emotional conditions for allergy, nutritional, mineral and vitamin, hormonal, or thyroid checkups. Further, assessment of life-style and social skills, degree of isolation, age related circumstances, and addictive behavior is necessary to understand a chronic condition and its treatment. In addition to in-patient care, these conditions may be treated by a knowledgeable therapist on an outpatient basis, with psychoactive drug therapy, or day treatment programs. This book is not intended to replace other treatments of these chronic conditions.

With these twelve assumptions in mind, let us proceed into the realm of emotional vitality. Consider this an exploration, as well as an opportunity to achieve mastery in the school of humanity.

NOTES

1. Mellody, Pia, *Facing Codependence*. San Francisco: Harper Row Publishers, 1989. (The best reference for understanding codependence. Read it.)

2. Bandler. R.; Grinder, John. *Reframing: NLP and the Transformation of Meaning*. Real People Press, 1982. A resource for understanding how our thinking affects our emotions and behavior. Full of insight and tools for change.)

3. Mellody (1989)

FURTHER READING:

1. Benson. Herbert. *The Mind-Body Effect*. Simon Schuster, New York, 1979; Berkeley, New York, 1980.

2. Bradshaw, John, *Homecoming*. NY: Bantam Books 1990. Inner child healing through visualization and words.

3. Cousins, Norman, *Anatomy of an Illness as Perceived by the Patient*. Norton, New York, 1979; Bantam, New York, 1981.

4. Fosshage, James L., and Paul Olsen. *Healing Implications for Psychotherapy*, Human Sciences Press. New York, 1978.

5. Hayes, Louise, *You Can Heal Your Life*. Santa Monica, Ca.: Hay House, 1984. (A terrific book for understanding the connection between the physical and emotional. Offers affirmations for healing oneself.)

6. Lappe, Francis Moore. *Diet for a Small Planet*. Random House, New York, 1971; Ballantine, New York, 1975. The definitive resource for approaching vegetarianism and why.

7. Lewis, Howard, and Martha E. Lewis. *Psychosomatics: How your Emotions Can Damage Your Health*. Viking, New York, 1972.

8. Locke, Steven and Mady Hornig-Rohan. *Mind and Immunity*. Institute for the Advancement of Health, New York, 1983.

9. Pelletier, Kenneth R. *Mind as Healer, Mind as Slayer*. Delacorte, New York, 1977; Delta, 1978.

10. Siegel, Bernie S., *Love, Medicine & Miracles*. NY: Harper & Row, 1986. Makes a good case for the miraculous powers of unconditional love on the immune system. Includes references to specific studies.

Chapter 3

GETTING DISTANCE WHEN WE NEED TO BE CALM: WHO IS RUNNING THINGS—CHILD OR ADULT SELF?

Being Out of Control vs. Getting in Charge

"By the time I realize I am out of control, it's too late to get in charge!" lamented Susan. Rose wept as she told me how helpless she felt knowing that her anxiety at anticipating her daughter's wedding would eventually rivet her to her seat so she could not be part of the reception line. Marie went to bed (with shame) for two days when her boss confronted her for not completing a task he assigned to her. And Mitch, who had been in therapy for a year, sobbed as he recounted how he had beaten his son and screamed at him when he refused to complete a chore, knowing as he did so that it was inappropriate and abusive. Being out of control of our feelings is scary and overwhelming. We can spend many years in quiet denial of our emotional suffering from mental confusion, a sense of isolation, or this or that ailment. Our emotions may erupt in uncontrolled and destructive ways—we may scream at our children or suffer a panic attack at a party. We find ourselves being offensive to others or incapacitated by our uncontrolled emotional attacks. Generally, those closest to us are the most capable of sending us running amuck, compass askew into the sea of lost rationality.

As mentioned before, emotions move through us as waves

of energy generating from our solar plexus and moving outwardly to our limbs and extremities. Using this metaphor, imagine the wave as having a source or trigger, then a gathering of energy and power, and finally, a cresting and gentle subsiding. Further, imagine being able to intervene at the source, or at least well before the cresting, to keep from catapulting into behavior that eludes our control.

While we may not be able to identify *what* is wrong in a given moment, we can learn to notice that *something* is wrong: tightening of the jaw, racing of the heart, shortness of breath, widening of the eyes, ringing in the ears. Or we may notice we are intellectualizing, analyzing or simply going numb. In that instant, we can change the direction of the events—either with a few deep breaths, counting to ten, a time-out to another room or outside for a few minutes, or just a statement that "something is wrong and I need to figure it out." Generally, leaving the stimulus will bring some relief and going to a safe place like your room may give a sense of safety. Once there is a break in the welling up of the wave, we can practice specific behaviors suggested in the next few chapters to become more in charge of our feeling behavior. If we can become more in balance with ourselves and our environment, make our feeling life a conscious process, and practice a few specific tools for catching the wave, we will be more able to circumvent offensive or self destructive behavioral extremes.

Inner Child vs. Adult Self

So who is acting so outrageously? She certainly isn't the serene, self assured, compassionate adult person who delivered baked goods to the local nursing home or who read bedtime stories to her child last night. Nor is he the person who clenched the multi-million dollar real estate deal or who handled a difficult employee conflict at the office. The person in question is more likely to be the three year old inside us whose development got arrested when s/he was left to take care of mom after one of dad's rages. Or perhaps it is the six year old who found refuge in the dark closet when left alone for hours. Again, maybe it is the sixteen year old who got date-raped after a party or the thirteen year old whose father reminded him daily that he would never amount to much.

Practicing the suggestions for embracing emotions will be difficult if you are unable to tell the difference between these two aspects of yourself. A general guideline for distinguishing between your adult and child self is that the child feels small and out of control, while the adult feels more centered and in charge. Generally, the child sends us into an addictive behavior such as overeating, overworking, television marathons, drug and alcohol abuse, or a shopping spree. The child aspect will not want to be logical or reasonable, nor will s/he necessarily be able to tell what motivated the behavior or what is needed to get centered again. In most cases, one can assume the child part of us is hurt, frightened, ashamed, or in need of comforting, attention, or recognition. We must get very good at attending to that inner child, lest she be compelled to get our attention by acting out.

Working With the Inner Child

Contacting and spending time with the inner child seems for many to be the most difficult treatment challenge. This is because we suffered so much neglect as children that we are unable to focus on the child. We have neither the attention for or the ability to visualize the child, nor the language to relate when we do. Work with this inner child as you would any child. Keep in mind that children need time to build trust and to know that you will wait until they are ready to come close or to tell you anything. They need to know you will be patient and supportive, that you will love them and protect them from harm. They need to be invited to join you, not with posturing or a demand, but with gentle encouragement and compassion. They must know it is no longer necessary to maintain walls or bravado; they can now share with you, and whoever else is available, their pain and fear, their loneliness and shame, their fury and feelings of powerlessness. They will look for consistency and for you to follow through—so don't make promises you won't keep.

Spending time daily with your inner child is the most important therapeutic work you can do toward healing your emotional wounds. Set a kitchen timer for three, then five, and eventually fifteen minutes to visualize and converse with your inner child. If visualizing is difficult for you, get out some old photographs of yourself as a child and animate them in your mind. You will find that the child's age may vary from teenage to three year old and then to six year old. That is perfectly all right. Just work with whatever age child comes to you. S/He is the one in need of your attention. You may notice one child may have more emotional impact than another. This simply means there is healing to do here and you must stay open to the data this child may offer you in terms of repressed memory or her response to you.

Our job is to grow this child up to functional adulthood. We have already known neglect and harsh treatment. That is the problem. So let us be more committed and conscientious in reparenting ourselves. Tell her you love her. Tell him you understand how frightened he is. Tell her she is beautiful, tell him he is enough. Tell her she doesn't have to do anything to earn your love, (yet she must act with respect toward herself, you and others). Tell him he is completely lovable even when he does things poorly. And then offer to show him how to do things better, with love and patience. Tell her you won't allow her to eat the whole chocolate cake because it will make her feel bad, but that she can have a small piece. Tell him that drinking alcohol is not the way to handle his feelings, and then tell him he can come to you or reach out to a safe person for comfort. Tell her she has a right to say "no," and then give her some guidelines about safe places and safe people, and about how being sexual is different from being loving. Tell him he doesn't have to be promiscuous and "macho" to be a man; show him that he can be safe with other men by discussing his fears or his needs. (Don't set him up by asking him to disclose with men who are unwilling to do the same. Find a safe place for him such as a therapy or self help group.)

After you work with your inner child for awhile, you will become more capable of deciding who is running things at any given moment. The goal, of course, is to have your adult self in charge, with your child reminding the adult about child-like qualities such as spontaneity, joyfulness, resiliency, forgiveness and tolerance. With the adult in charge most often, we will have greater dominion over our feelings. Remember, too, that we will act irresponsibly at times. No need for alarm. This just means we have more growing to do and that we are wonderfully imperfect!

FURTHER READING

1. Abrams, Jeremiah, ed. *Reclaiming the Inner Child*, Los Angeles, Ca.: Jeremy P. Tarcher, Inc. Thirty seven articles from leading experts in psychology.

2. Faber, Adele and Mazlisch. Elaine, *How to Talk So Kids Will Listen and Listen So Kids Will Talk*. Avon Books, 1982. Good practice for talking with your inner child.

3. Pollard, John. *Self Parenting*. Millbrae, CA: Generic Human Studies Publishing, 1987. A guide for reparenting the inner child.

    4. Taylor, Cathryn, *The Inner Child Workbook*, LA: Jeremy P. Tarcher. Inc. A step by step guide to inner child work.

    5. Wholey, Dennis, *Becoming Your Own Parent*, NY: Doubleday, 1988. Interviews and contributions from voices in the field of codependence.

Chapter 4

GUIDELINES FOR PRACTICING EMOTIONAL BEHAVIOR

____ 1. Use this book as a checklist. As you feel you understand and can assimilate the information in each section, check it off. If you get stuck you probably need more information. Pursue some of the suggested readings or have a conversation with someone about the concept.

____ 2. Choose one emotion at a time to practice. Standard procedure might include assessing how this emotion is a problem for you or those around you. What consequences are you experiencing or how are you acting in the extreme around this feeling? What do you usually do when you feel this particular emotion? How do you avoid the feeling? What emotion do you usually use to mask this feeling? What would you like to be able to do?

____ 3. Seek opportunities to feel. See your feelings as gifts, bringing you empowerment, wholeness, a sense of being alive, and the ability to connect with others. If feeling numb is a prevalent condition for you, seek out emotionally poignant movies, novels, news items, etc., and give yourself permission to weep or laugh aloud. If everything hits you with tremendous intensity, seek opportunities that will help you to get distance. Find alone time. Take a walk with a friend. Get away for the weekend to a quiet retreat. Gain dominion over your emotional state and behavior by orchestrating the circumstances in which you have them.

___ 4. Require quiet, undistracted time to focus on your-self each day. It is easy to make the chores, the kids, the job the reason for your lack of time alone. My experience is that there will *always* be something else to do or someone else's needs to fulfill. Even if it is fifteen minutes of quiet meditation or journal writing, take time for you. I find that if I don't, there isn't much for me to give to others, anyway. Turn off the television. Close your eyes and be still. Notice what you experience in your body and where. Ask yourself what that sensation might be trying to tell you. Listen.

___ 5. If you cannot identify what you are feeling, guess at it. Just give it a feeling name and note where in your body you feel it. Later, as you become adept at feeling language and self awareness, you may want to redefine or refine more specifically those unknowns. Ask someone if what they feel is similar or in a similar physical place. Don't be afraid to commit a word to your experience, you will eventually know if it is correct.

___ 6. Seek out models. Children are especially spontane-ous with emotions such as joy or pain. Find others you consider healthy around particular feelings and observe what they do or don't do. Pay attention to their attitudes or spiritual values, their self care practices, and notice how they receive comfort or support. You may even want to interview them.

___ 7. Practice affirmations. One of the highest teachings in the spiritual literature is the idea that we create much of our own reality by our attitudes and beliefs. Kinesiology proves that just the suggestion of weakness cause weakness (Try this: have someone resist as you push firmly on their outstretched arm, then have him/her repeat aloud several times "I am weak" as they resist you again. You will find that a person is unable to maintain the same level of strength while repeating this phrase.) Children are given thousands of hours of negative messages in some families of origin. As you grow up, you may find yourself repeating these messages in the form of self doubt, self criticism, or pessimism. To free yourself from these destructive messages, replace them with more positive and healthful premises.

But, you say, if you could remember to say something positive you would! Practice. Practice. Practice. If you consciously embrace affirming self talk, you will be less likely to berate yourself unconsciously. For each shaming phrase running through your head, replace it with its opposite. ("I am intelligent and I have something important to share in my writing," rather than "Boy am I stupid. Nothing I say is important, so why bother writing it?") Then, repeat this new phrase as often as it occurs to you. Repeat it until you believe it. Try not to qualify your affirmation with negatives, maybes, or soons. State your positive quality as if it already exists. The truth is, it does exist. You simply have forgotten or were never told how wonderful you are!

_____ 8. Make the recovery of your emotional life a priority. Commit to your own growth and take time to focus on yourself. Use the examples in this book daily to practice wholeness. Get a physical examination, revamp your diet to include more fresh fruit and vegetables and less meat, read every day, write in your journal, meditate or pray, get out for exercise, spend time with your inner child. Commit financially to getting healthy, be it attending a health club, spiritual intensive, or therapeutic workshop. Change friends if your old ones don't support what you are trying to do. Take a class in creative expression, such as painting, sculpture, chorale, drama, public speaking or writing. Get a massage. Go dancing in a smoke free environment. Join a spiritual study group. Ask yourself daily, "What am I doing today that will help me to grow emotionally?"

_____ 9. Attend to your language. Eliminate words like **can't, I don't know, maybe, yes but, why can't you....** Use words like **I will, I won't, I have a right to, I feel..., I believe or I think...** Notice your tone of voice—do you sound whiny or negative, helpless or dependent, gruff or defiant? Notice how you stand (shoulders rounded, chest sunken, head hanging?) as it will affect how you project yourself into the world, as well as how you greet change. Stand tall and project your voice. Often language can prevent you from achieving a goal or finding empowerment. Be bold and courageous as you seek balance in your emotional life. Act confidently until you become confident.

_____ 10. Have purpose in what you do. Ask yourself if what you are doing meets an emotional need, expresses some aspect of your value system or philosophy, or serves others. Work at a job that is meaningful to you for one of these reasons. If this is not possible right now, use your job as an opportunity to get you where you want to be—through promotion, further education or saving money. At home, live your values, be it through recycling, community service, conserving water, or growing your own vegetables. Work hard at what you do, but not too hard. When work and purposefulness become compulsive or obsessive, they are unhealthy activities. Having the power of your beliefs and values behind what you do generate motivation and creativity. You will feel better, too.

_____ 11. Seek out your Higher Power. Having a source greater than yourself for strength or unconditional love can be extremely helpful when trying new and perhaps scary behavior. There are many ways to achieve a connection with a Higher Power. Read spiritual books, daily meditations or inspirational phrases. Attend a church, temple or ashram. Spend time in prayer, meditation or silence. Create your own rituals or find someone who can help you with this (use your discretion and make sure your rituals are for love and service to others, and that they never involve death or blood sacrifice). Spend time in nature—walk in the park or the forest, go river rafting or backpacking, swim in a mountain lake or wade in the ocean, paint the flora of the desert or the birds of the jungle. Visit a National Park in the off season when there are fewer tourists. Hug a tree or care for a pet animal. There is divinity in all things. Once you are convinced of this, you will likely see the interconnection of life, and you will know that you are an integral part—unique and invaluable. How can one feel shame or joylessness about that?

____ 12. Create and maintain good physical, sexual, emotional, spiritual and intellectual boundaries. A boundary is the experience of having a protective shield around the body and of being able to remain unaffected by another's perception. Boundaries separate what is yours and what is another's. Behind the physical boundary, you remain safe from physical and sexual touch, determine for yourself when you want to be touched, and give others the right to decide this, too. The emotional boundary helps you to hold onto your beliefs, thoughts or feelings despite what others say or do and allows others their reality also. With boundaries, you set limits with others and act more responsibly for yourself.[1*]

Visualize a protective barrier, made of any material (including light weight, see-through, solid-as-a-concrete-wall space-age substance!) you can feel safe behind. See it beyond your body about two to three feet, containing all of who you are, protecting you from others. Now, notice that you can move that boundary in and out, depending on who you want near you. Repeat to yourself that you have a right to protect yourself and contain who you are. Remind yourself that what other people think and say about you is not necessarily true about you at all. What others think or believe is about what they have created in their minds from their perceptions which can be interpretations, biases, or misunderstood observations, beliefs, and historical experiences. See the boundary as separating you from others, so you can know what you think or believe. You control what comes in and whether you want it to change your beliefs. Keeping other's perceptions out requires distancing yourself. If you were to meet a person who is convinced that you are a tree in disguise, you might say to yourself. "Isn't that an interesting thought." So might you respond to someone convinced that you are selfish because you refuse to make one more meal without help.

Practice using boundaries with everyone, including parents, siblings, spouses, teachers, employers and grocery store clerks. Play with your boundaries in line at the movie, on the sidewalk, or in an airplane. You will find some situations impossible for getting enough distance, such as an elevator. Practice turning your body, looking up or away. Do whatever it takes to feel safe. You may even ask someone to step back or to refrain from touching you. This practice may feel awkward at first, but you will feel better as you notice how much more comfortable you are. As you honor other's boundaries you will notice them getting more comfortable with you, as well.

You are worth every moment you spend seeking growth. Nothing can be any more important than your emotional health and well being. You are the creator of your life now, and you can choose wholeness. Herein are some tools. You must bring the determination and caring.

NOTES

Mellody, Pia, *Boundaries*, an audiotape series from Mellody Enterprises, AZ. An excellent resource for a thorough discussion on boundaries.

PART II

THE EMOTIONS:
RECLAIMING OUR HUMANITY

SPIRITUAL PAIN

..."*We can fly! We can become butterflies! There's nothing at the top and it doesn't matter!*"

As he heard his own message he realized how he had misread the instinct to get high. To get to the "top" he must fly, not climb.

Stripe looked at each caterpillar inebriated with joy that there could be a butterfly inside.

But the reaction was worse than before. He saw fear in the eyes.

They didn't stop to listen or speak.

This happy, glorious news was too much to take—too good to be true.

And if it wasn't true?

The hope that lit up the pillar dimmed.

All seemed confused and unreal.

The way down was immensely long.

The vision of the butterfly faded.

Doubt flooded Stripe.

The pile took on horrible dimensions.

He struggled on—barely—blindly.

It seemed wrong to give up believing—yet believing seemed impossible.

A crawler sneered, "How could you swallow such a story?

Our life is earth and climbing. Look at us worms!

We couldn't be butterflies inside.

Make the best of it and enjoy caterpillar living!"

"*Perhaps he's right,*" *sighed Stripe.*

"*I haven't any proof.*

Did I only make it up because I needed it so much?"

And in pain he continued down searching for those eyes which would let him whisper,

"*I saw a butterfly—there can be more to life.*"

> *hope for the flowers*
> *by trina paulus*

Chapter 5

SPIRITUAL PAIN

I realize that the premise for this chapter may be contro-
versial. People generally don't like to be told how to think
about spiritual matters. My intention is certainly not to offend
or turn away the reader from looking at the issue of spiritual
pain. Rather, I present the following ideas because my experience of this type of pain has been real and a source of a great
deal of searching for me. In talking with others who have
wrestled with faith, transcendence, and their corporeal experience of union, I have determined a common thread. Perhaps
it is an interpretation I alone make regarding spiritual pain.
However, when I ask people if this fits for them, they often will
agree. You must decide for yourself if this is true for you. If it
isn't true for you, you may still find useful guidance in the
section on Tools for Recovering and Practicing Spiritual Pain.

Spiritual Pain is the experience of profound loss, almost
agony, related specifically to the awareness of our separation
from the divine source of unconditional love. This pain is a
rudimentary experience in the infant's prenatal life and is an
integral part of becoming human. As our souls descend into
the physical form during gestation, severing union with Creator, we find ourselves constricted by the physical form and
limited in our ability to give and receive unconditional love.
We have fallen from grace. We awaken to the world already

with a grievous sense of being alone and a deep longing for reunion with the Purest Love.

We come into the world needy, innocent about the rules of being in the world, and trusting that we will be the center of our parent's loving universe. The memory of divine loving is fresh; our experience suggests that life on earth will be similar to what we recently left. However, by nature, humans are limited in their ability to love unconditionally and so the infant/soul lands in the hands of sometimes unavailable or cruel parents. We feel a deeper loss.

Some babies who have had the good fortune of being born in a loving and wholesome way (such as in water or through a home birth) may not be so wounded by the initial birth trauma. However, we all grow up with human parents and we discover sometime that, though theirs can be the most wonderful and balanced loving, it is still not the same as "spiritual" union. We spend the rest of our lives seeking this union and occasionally experience moments of it with family, friends, romantic relationships, or, if we are fortunate enough, with our Higher Selves through nature or guidance from a spiritual teacher. The search becomes even more critical if the experiences of childhood are less than nurturing.

As I work with people to heal childhood wounds, I find that they will drop into a kind of pain that is different from other pain; it is deeper and more difficult to hold in the body. This pain is experienced in the solar plexus, heart and eyes. There are no pictures associated with this pain and it is sometimes stimulated by a loving affirmation or the feeling of safety for the first time. Spiritual pain is a mixture of remembering what we had sometime in our soul's memory, realizing what we have longed for all our lives, and knowing what we have never had in our human experience. Spiritual pain underlies all other emotions and compels us to seek union with that which is beyond this world, the world of spirit. In finding that union, we rise above the human condition and become free of limited beliefs, which are the root of emotional disturbance. When spiritual pain is mastered, emotions become more easily managed.

There are a few variations of spiritual pain:

Anguish and *despair* compel us to grieve deep within ourselves and to seek understanding of life's meaning.

Utter aloneness compels us to find union with someone or something else. We often mistake this for a longing for human connection.

Pain-filled joy is a mixture of sadness for the loss of not having had a feeling of being loved unconditionally and the joy of experiencing this love. This often comes when we get affirmed, when we share ourselves and find acceptance, or when we realize we are an integral part of the beauty around us. This is the experience of spiritual understanding and grace.

What goes wrong when we don't feel our spiritual pain: We may:
-numb ourselves with addictions, too many activities or people
-fill our lives with money or things as a perceived source of fulfillment
-become hopeless and despairing regarding life's trialS
-see ourselves as victims, punished for our human failings
-avoid responsibility
-become suicidal, feeling without purpose or direction
-become hardened or unsympathetic to another's suffering
-lack compassion and joyfulness
-become controlling of others

What can go wrong physically when we don't express our spiritual pain:
-cancer, especially of throat, brain, lung
-brain tumors
-autoimmune disease (the body becomes allergic to itself)
-leukemia and other blood diseases (loss of life force)
-addiction related diseases (suicide by default)
-thyroid problems (life's longing for itself)
-multiple sclerosis (loss of body control forces us to give over that control to a power greater than ourselves)
-stiffness in joints, paralysis

TOOLS FOR RECOVERING AND PRACTICING SPIRITUAL PAIN

____ 1. Familiarize yourself with what hurts you. When you look at the losses you experienced in your life, notice if the longing for connection or union underlies the pain you felt. Go back and look again. This time, for the sake of experimentation, superimpose a picture of loving hands reaching down from the heavens, holding you through the loss. Notice how different this feels. Be open to the possibility that what happened is part of a plan which can only be seen in retrospect.

When your secular work is in progress or completed, spiritual work can be identified. Hopefully, as you practice Pain, you will discover that the sacred underlies all you do. If you understand this idea, then life becomes an intricate and exquisite unfolding of choices that takes you into the realm of divine humanity.

____ 2. Contact your inner child daily. Inner child work is

essential to understanding spiritual pain. The child in us feels both the loss of a loving human parent and the loss of the divine Mother/Father. The work involves reparenting the child in a loving, nurturing, respectful and consistent way, and also re-educating child and adult self about God, Higher Power, the Divine, or Spirit. Your child self will likely need much affirming about her preciousness, the miracle of his birth and survival, the joy you feel about her childlike (god-like) qualities, or the grace he brings to your life. The inner child must understand both cognitively and emotionally her/his part in the universe and this understanding begins with you. You reflect to the child this knowledge by your consistency, affirmation and loving treatment. As you seek understanding and practice love for yourself and your inner child, your soul will remember its origin and purpose and you will begin to experience spiritual pain.

_____ 3. Seek understanding of your spirituality. The mind must be satisfied in its quest for "knowledge" about the possibilities, probabilities, and potentialities of the spiritual. These can be found in hundreds of contemporary writings, from sacred psychology, near death experiences, and psychosynthesis to mysticism, shamanism, and mythology. You may even seek understanding in physics or history. Studying the lives of prophets and saints, wise men and ascetics reveals the human experience of spiritual pain. As with any new yearning, spiritual search requires time, attention and disciplined practice to bring forth its fruit. Study hard and long the teachings you find. Ask questions of knowledgeable people. Don't expect the ground to move or the oceans to part because you have prayed a few times or read a book or two on religion. Relationship with the divine takes more than this. Unwavering commitment, intense longing, and absolute faith are just the beginning. Just getting to these qualities takes a great deal of effort.

_____ 4. Assume that you have spiritual pain. Create a daily routine that includes spiritual practice such as prayer or meditation, reading or writing inspirational ideas, ritual or ceremony, church service or community service, singing or chanting spiritual songs, being in or serving nature. You may simply need to sit and weep, staying with the pain until it passes.

In the separation of church and state, spirituality has been separated from daily life. This is evident in the designation of one day per week to be "religious," such as Saturday or Sunday. We have been separated from our inner life, and away from a sense of family or community. Our ability to feel a connection with or responsibility for the planet becomes impaired. Other cultures practice prayer or meditation several times per day, ceremony and rituals several days per week or month, and have yearly religious celebrations that span several days or weeks. Some Native Americans for example, give thanks each morning as they greet the sun with reverence and awe. They express gratitude to all their relations, including the animals and birds, plants and trees, clouds and rain, wind and seeds. This daily reminder keeps the relationship with all life conscious and foremost.

_____ 5. Treat your body well. The physical form is a manifestation of the spiritual will. As you open your heart and mind to a higher level of functioning in your spiritual work, you also must make the vessel pure. Good hygiene and a diet with little or no meat, alcohol, caffeine, or nicotine, and high in vegetables, fruits and grains will allow the body to function more efficiently. Being physical in some work or recreation activity builds strength and suppleness and tones the internal organs. Perspiration clears the pores and detoxifies the skin (as does skin brushing). Of course, abstaining from anything toxic to the body or potentially addictive is essential.

Health and well being in the body can be greatly augmented

by visualizing your body as whole several times a day. This is accomplished by sitting quietly and comfortably for a few minutes. Starting at the top of your head and moving down through the body, imagine your organs, bones, circulatory system, and even your cells radiating energy, the life force or chi, and creating perfect harmony. Fill your body, as you complete this exercise, with your love and appreciation. Take some deep breaths and take comfort in the body's ability to function wholly.

____ 6. Use your mind as an ally. Free yourself of negative thoughts and eliminate mental laziness. Negative and lazy thinking result from too much reliance on others to think for us, excessive television time and ingesting chemicals. Be curious, dedicated in your quest for understanding and experience, and act on the insight that comes to you. Reward yourself with compliments, social events or special spiritual books for creative ideas and time spent seeking spiritual answers. When you understand a particular route to your Higher Self, avoid backsliding into habits and thinking patterns that keep you in the intensity of emotional extremes by making spiritual work part of your daily routine, reading spiritual literature, gathering with like-minded people, or saying "no" to upsetting thoughts.

Develop the quality of detachment. This does not mean to lack caring. On the contrary, caring is an essential ingredient to becoming spiritually whole. To detach means to cultivate a quality of loving like divine love. This is a little like having compassion and respect without counting on or requiring a particular outcome or reciprocal act. Detachment allows life to unfold as we remain free of needing to control. This is a wonderful quality that helps to stabilize emotions and keep us out of extremes.

One of my pet peeves has always been that the things that taste the best or are the most fun to do turn out to be detrimental to me. Of course, I have also discovered that the less I do those "fun" things, the less I want to do them. They simply are no longer fun to do. Granted, this may be a function of getting older, but I feel too that I have grown to enjoy and appreciate feeling "top notch" and unadulterated.

Carl Japikse urges people to develop "productivity and self-sufficiency...generosity, helpfulness, good will...cooperation, humility, wisdom...responsibility, purposefulness, altruism, and dedication." (1) With these qualities balanced with moderation, the spirit within us finds expression and direction.

___ 7. Do whatever it takes to master your addictive behavior. Addictions keep the mind obsessed with activities that are rarely in our best interest. Abstinence is addiction's greatest enemy. You will know if you are abusing or becoming addicted to someone or something if you are unable to stop doing an activity, ingesting a food or drug, or being with someone without experiencing discomfort and fear. A reasonable period of abstinence is one week to three months. If you think you may have difficulty abstaining, get help. Know that there are many effective ways to freedom.

The Twelve Step programs such as Alcoholics Anonymous, Codependents Anonymous, Overeaters Anonymous, Sex and Love Addicts Anonymous, or Adult Children of Alcoholics are all self help community based programs where people can get support and direction for recovering from compulsive behaviors. The steps are designed to reveal your spirituality. Finding a good addictions counselor or therapist can be invaluable. Consider an inpatient treatment program designed to help with the withdrawal period while providing group support and wholesome life-style changes.

Many people attempt to master their addictions by simply stopping the behavior. Chances are high for relapse unless there are qualitative changes made in life-style, relationships, or work habits. Getting to the underlying reasons that drive addictive behavior will often bring about positive changes. Grieving and building new communication tools can add tremendous support to your quest for wholeness.

Relief in the area of addictions is critical to the development and cultivation of a spiritual life. Remember that spiritual pain underlies all of our emotions and that it compels us to evolve to our highest functioning. So you see that addictive thinking keeps us bound to lower functioning and in darkness. Intensity keeps us bound to fear, anger, jealousy, and shame and away from divine love.

____ 8. Spend time alone with yourself. Learning to be comfortable with solitude is of utmost importance. The experience of being alone in the universe is the root of spiritual pain. In moments of abandonment or betrayal, we experience loneliness and may tap that primordial wound in the soul's memory. Coming into the world was a little like being three and gleefully running from daddy's "gonna gitcha" only to turn around and find Daddy not there any more. We have lovingly been guided here and left to fend for ourselves with little understanding and direction, or so it seems. The truth is that we are given guidance, we just haven't learned to listen. Solitude free of distractions assures time to hear what the inner voice directs. This listening also may ignite the flame of self love and bring forth creative energy. We move from being pained about our aloneness to being more alive and joyful. At the very least, solitude may bring the experience of love. Now who wouldn't want that?

____ 9. Love as often as you can. As you will see in Chapter 6, love can be expressed in many ways. Having compassion for and serving others are the highest virtues you practice in your quest for spiritual evolution. Jesus gave the world a human example of kindness, respect and compassion. He taught us that giving time, attention and good will to others can heal.

The planet and its occupants could use a major dose of loving attention. This involves taking your familial love to a group or community level, and as a group or community to a planetary level. If every human being acted in loving compassion for another human, animal or plant at least once daily, we would begin to heal our ravaged earth. Equally important is the necessity to eliminate greed and lust for power while developing the virtues of generosity and acquiescence. We must practice harmonious co-existence politically, economically, and spiritually.

Spiritual pain will transform into joy as we cultivate integrity. This means being honest with ourselves and others, being caring and compassionate toward others, having positive intention toward all life, and becoming whole human beings. Spiritual integrity involves congruence on every level of being—physical, intellectual, emotional, and as a planetary community. Native Americans consider what the impact of every community decision they make will be on seven future generations. We must follow such examples very soon if we are going to survive.

___ 10. Be courageous in expressing your spiritual joy. Others may not understand or want to participate in your joy. Human beings tend to be afraid of what they do not understand. Someone who understands very little of joy or spirituality may be judgemental or harsh. Simply note that this is not someone open to what you have to share and go on about experiencing and expressing your bliss.

I like to tell the story of a dear man who lives in the small town where I live in the Sierra foothills. Everyone knows Smithy because of his peculiar dress, his joyful way, and his love of God. We figure he is in his seventies because of his flowing white hair and his deeply wrinkled skin. He wears colorful mismatched clothing—reds and purples, shorts over long pants, bright colored scarves for ties and a red patent leather rain coat. He is always the first to dance to street bands and leads the carolers at Christmas. He is sweet to babies and children and radiates warmth and smiles to all he passes. His spiritual joy is evident as he raises his arms in praise and gratitude, a smile on his lips, as he contemplates a simple cup of coffee in the local cafe. He never harms anyone, brings only joy and curiosity to those of us he meets. This is a man oblivious to others' judgment of him, who has found a way to be in the world, alone with his Master.

The expression of your spiritual joy may look odd to another. You may even look suspiciously strange. Whenever you have any intense feeling, you must be conscious of others and respectful in your self expression. Timing and moderation are essential if you want to fit in and be a part of society. If joy is too much to contain, I encourage you to find others who understand and can join you in the bliss. I also encourage you to find ways at home to express this spiritual joy. Let yourself go, rejoice in the hard work that has brought you to this joy, and give back in gratitude and love what you have received.

"And when you bemoan the suffering you have long endured...
Know that the waiting seed needs a struggle to break through its prison of
soil...or it can never grow.
Learn that nothing is ever really dead.
And if you strive, you can escape any prison.
But effort is always needed.
For, without the problem of reaching for the sunlight..
Every seed would remain a seed.
So, resent not your difficulties in the jungle
Or your loneliness in the desert.
For each state teaches its own lesson.
Learn from the kaleidoscope of experience that colors your life...
You need everything that happens to you...."

Keepers of the Earth
Kristin Zambucka

AFFIRMATIONS FOR
EMBRACING SPIRITUAL PAIN/JOY

Many people have been terribly spiritually abused. In childhood the idea of God was used to punish or control the child's behavior. Consequently, the experience of anything religious or spiritual became unpalatable and scary, driving one further into spiritual pain. Affirmations will serve to reframe this dilemma, clearing the slate for a new definition of the spiritual or religious. I have intentionally not addressed the "religious" because the heart of spiritual pain is beyond dogma and philosophy, which are the realm of religion. Spiritual pain is the experience of being caught between humanity and divinity, being both and neither. Use these affirmations or create your own to relieve your spiritual pain:

I am first and foremost a child of Divine Love.
I have a right to understand God or Higher Power as I choose.
I see in the perfection of my imperfection a divine plan.
The pain I feel in being separate indicates my longing for a relationship with my Higher Self.
I have a right to spiritual joy.
I embrace right understanding and trust my intuition and discretion.
I recognize as truth what resonates as truth within me.
In loving and serving others I express my higher nature.
There are no cosmic rules against seeking understanding, only support.
My soul expresses itself in all loving acts

NOTES

Japikse, Carl. *The Light Within Us*. Columbus. OH: Ariel Press, 1987. Pg 92.

FURTHER READING

1. Gawain, Shakti. *Creative Visualization*. NY: Bantam Books, 1978. A terrific resource for using visualization.

2. Japikse. Carl. *The Light Within Us*. Columbus. OH: Ariel Press, 1987. A terrific resource for the serious aspirant who is unafraid of guidance from an eclectic source. Based on the teaching of Patanjali and Jesus.

3. Ferrucci, Piero. *Inevitable Grace*. Los Angeles, CA: Jeremy P. Tarcher, Inc. 1991. Brings insight to the lives of spiritual geniuses and the difficulties they faced. Good inspiration.

4. Grof, Stanislav and Grof, Christina eds. *Spiritual Emergency*. Los Angeles, Ca: Jeremy P. Tarcher, Inc. 1989. Addresses relationships between spiritual crisis and madness and healing.

5. ———, *The Stormy Search for the Self*. Los Angeles, Ca: Jeremy P. Tarcher, Inc. 1990. More on the idea of spiritual emergency.

6. Fields. Rick; Taylor, Peggy; Weyler, Rex; Ingrasci, Rick. *Chop Wood, Carry Water*. Los Angeles. CA: Los Angeles, CA: Jeremy P. Tarcher, 1984.

7. Hixon, Lex, *Coming Home*. Los Angeles. Ca: Jeremy P. Tarcher, Inc. 1989, 1978. A study into the possibilities of spiritual evolution available to all of us. A good beginning for seekers of understanding.

8. Zukav, Gary, *The Dancing Wu Li Masters*. NY: Wm. Morrow & Co., 1979. A classic in the study of spirituality.

9. ———, *The Seat of the Soul*. New York, NY: Simon & Schuster Inc., 1990. I think this should be required reading for everyone.

LOVE

...The fox gazed at the little prince, for a long time.

"Please—tame me!" he said.

"I want to, very much," the little prince replied.

"But I have not much time. I have friends to discover and a great many things to understand."

"One only understands the things that one tames," said the fox. "Men have no more time to understand anything, They buy things all ready made at the shops. But there is no shop anywhere where one can buy friendship, and so men have no friends anymore. If you want a friend, tame me...."

...So the little Prince tamed the fox. And when the hour of his departure drew near—

"Ah," said the fox, "I shall cry."

"It is your own fault," said the little prince. "I never wished you any sort of harm; but you wanted me to tame you..."

"Yes, that is so," said the fox.

"Then it has done you no good at all!"

"It has done me good," said the fox, "because of the color of the wheat fields...."

..."Goodbye," he said.

"Goodbye," said the fox. "And now here is my secret, a very simple secret: It is only with the heart that one can see rightly; what is essential is invisible to the eye".

"What is essential is invisible to the eye," the little prince repeated, so that he would be sure to remember .

"It is the time you have wasted for your rose that makes your rose so important."

"It is the time I have wasted for my rose—" said the little prince, so that he would be sure to remember.

"Men have forgotten this truth," said the fox.

"But you must not forget it. You become responsible, forever, for what you have tamed. You are responsible for your rose..."

"I am responsible for my rose," the little prince repeated, so that he would be sure to remember.

The Little Prince
Antoine de Saint Exupery

Chapter 6

LOVE

Love is a state of well-being arising out of a sense of being valued and connected with others or a Higher Power. When we feel safe and have loving models, our capacity for loving is limitless. Human beings are inherently lovable and capable of loving. From love, we create great things—a koan, the Brooklyn Bridge, a symphony, the Peace Quilt or a child. From love, we protect and defend. A mother's caution or a soldier's pride in his country's flag generates security, loyalty, courage and hope. Misguided love can even destroy, as in jealousy, national conquest, or missionary zeal.

Our earliest experience of love comes with attention to our physical needs in infancy—the predictability of a response when we cry. As our vision clears, we notice joy on our mother's face, reflecting a welcome from the physical world. Later, father's pride in our accomplishments motivates us to please. We learn parental love and self care from those who care for us. In school, friendship becomes the arena for love's expression. We learn about sharing, loyalty, and compassion for others. Later as we develop sexually, we find tenderness, affection and flirtation. As our self confidence becomes firmly rooted and we discover the rest of the world, we experience admiration, respect, pride and brotherhood. From the wounds of rejection, lost romantic love, or shame, we may seek the safety and limitless compassion of love's source. In spiritual discovery, love may be experienced as faith, devotion, serenity, rapture or ecstasy.

In addition to these experiences, love is expressed in tenderness, care giving, focused attention, physical affection, a smile, gifts of time, labor or money. Sex is not the same as love, but can be an expression of love if it is given between consenting adults who share an emotional commitment. Otherwise, sex is lust's expression and can be a misguided attempt to get love. See Lust.

Love is experienced around the heart, with a feeling of fullness, lightness, even giddiness. Intense love can feel like waves of ecstatic energy pulsating through the body, much like the electrical current surging from socket to lamp. When inspired by a thing of beauty or awe, tears of joy may arise.

Whenever we experience even a moment of true unconditional love, we will most likely seek it relentlessly until we feel it again. Consequently, there may be a tendency to assign our loving joyfulness to someone else, thereby giving away the power to own the true source of love—our spirituality.

There are many variations of love:

Friendship, brotherhood, loyalty, compassion, truth, fondness— compel us to be connected, to include another and to forgive.

Tenderness, affection, flirtation—compel us to touch, kiss or caress.

Admiration, respect, pride, honor—compel us to hold another in high regard.

Devotion, adoration, rapture, spiritual ecstasy—compel us to place another above ourselves and other things.

(Remember: Sex is not a variation of love. See Lust)

What goes wrong when we don't feel our love:
We may:
-feel shut down or disconnected from others and the
 world
-rely on anger to get us through life's daily tasks
-feel dull, joyless, bored
-despair, feel hopeless
-blame others
-lack purpose, ask "What's it all about?"
-rely on lust or sexual intercourse to connect
-feel envy or jealousy
-have many negative life experiences such as repeated
 accidents
-isolate ourselves
-become insensitive, abusive to others, even mean

*What can go wrong physically when we don't express
our love:*
-severe debilitating illnesses may arise, causing de
 pendence on others for care
-heart problems (from a broken heart)
-throat or thyroid problems (from the longing to
 connect)
-uterine, cervical, reproductive, or genital problems
 (with the inappropriate expression of sexual love)
-stiffness, arthritis (from not acting on our love)
-weight retention or gain (to protect or armor)
-cancer (from not sharing ourselves with others)

TOOLS FOR RECOVERING
AND PRACTICING LOVE

____ 1. Hate something. Maybe it is the colors of the rose and red flowers that clash in the vase or the trashy cars in your neighbor's yard. If you can hate something, even with passion, so too will you be able to love something—with passion.

____ 2. Attend to your body. Eat well: more fresh fruits and vegetables, whole grains, water and simple foods; less meat, fat, salt, dairy or processed foods. Reduce or eliminate the use of alcohol, caffeine, nicotine, and sugar. You will find even small amounts of these powerful chemicals are unnecessary after awhile. Drinking fluids with meals dilutes the digestive juices and slows digestive action, causing problems in the stomach and colon. If drinking liquids other than water is necessary, try spritzers of fruit juice and carbonated water, vegetable juice, or herbal teas. Eliminate all illegal drugs and be cautious about taking prescription drugs. Too many for too long can be dangerous and create dependency. Bathe frequently: at least once a day if you labor physically or four times per week if you are more sedentary. Exercise moderately: walk, bicycle, swim, take dance aerobics, lift weights, practice yoga. Exercise three to four times per week. Wear attractive, comfortable, clothing that breathes: natural fibers such as cotton, wool, silk, ramie, or linen. Attend to the color of your clothing; if it doesn't feel right or comfortable to wear what you laid out the night before, choose something that feels better. Pay attention to the texture of your clothing: it should be soothing to the skin, smell good, and fall comfortably. Act as though you love your body until you do.

____ 3. Do something special now and then for yourself. Take yourself to a special play, ballet, ball game, out to dinner or lunch. Buy yourself something you want, and make it something you don't necessarily need. Take an afternoon to laze in the park or read a good book. Have a hot bubble bath with candles and classical music. Send a bouquet of flowers to your house with a card to yourself inscribed "You are truly special. I love you!" Express love to yourself as you would to another. Make your own little universe enough for now and fill it with all the love you wish another would give you. If you can truly honor yourself you will be more able to receive appreciation from or honor another.

_____ 4. Create something. When creating you are expressing your deepest self and bringing something unique to the world. Plant petunias in the spring or bake a special cake for someone you care about. Write a poem, story, or song. Express yourself through a painting, drawing or doodle; a sculpture, clay figure, or mask, a dance, ritual, or simple musical instrument; a new dress, painted sweatshirt, or crocheted hat; a table, bookshelf, or tree house; a pea patch for the neighborhood, playground for the school, or recycling center for the community. Raise money to help the homeless, AIDS patients, or victims of oppression. Whatever you choose to do, see it as an opportunity to express yourself—to express your love to yourself or to another. Be mindful not to choose something too difficult or overwhelming; you will want to avoid resentment or martyrdom.

_____ 5. Do something for someone else. Prepare a meal and deliver it; do a friend's ironing or fix a neighbor's car; volunteer a few hours per week at the local nursing home or women's shelter; send a special card or a bouquet of flowers— just because; give of yourself, your time and your attention to another. Sometimes just listening is enough. Do something you know would be appreciated even if it isn't the most comfortable thing for you to do; sing her a love song or wear a sexy fru fru for him even if it is cold. Be careful to give to others because it feels good to you to do so, not because you "should" or "better." And be sure to balance this with Number

3 above.

____ 6. Find something in each person to love or appreciate. Know that most people have a positive intention behind their behavior, even if they appear mean or disrespectful. Smile at people. Offer compliments or appreciation for another's work or behavior. Do this frequently and sincerely, but don't overdo. Occasionally, practice saying, "I care for you" or "I love you." Offer to treat someone to a ballet, a nice dinner, a special sports event, etc. as a way of showing your gratitude for who they are or what they give to you. (And graciously accept being treated when it is offered.) Remembering to tell someone something you liked is harder than complaining when something goes wrong. Train your brain to sort for the good stuff, too.

____ 7. When you are in a romantic partnership, ask each other for and provide each other a list of things you would like the other to do for you. The most common complaint I hear from women about their men is that they aren't "romantic." The most common male complaint is that she isn't interested in sex enough. What is "romantic" or "enough?" Only you know what these things mean to you. Telling another what you like or want is often one of the most difficult things to do, but also one of the most satisfying. And it *does* count if you get what you ask for.

____ 8. Give love without any expectation. Leo Buscalia says, "If one waits to love only until he is certain of receiving equal love in return, he may wait forever. Indeed, if he loves with any expectation at all, he will surely be disappointed eventually, for it's not likely that most people can meet all of his needs even if their love for him is great." (l) Give of yourself because it gives you pleasure to do so.

You may not understand another's language of love. Ask what your partner does as the expression of his/her love. Then accept that what your partner does to express love for you is given with good intention; even if it doesn't match your yearning. Be thankful for the toaster or snow shovel, then gently remind your partner of those things that would also be meaningful to you. Make a list of things your partner does to show you love, and then ask him/her to add the other things s/he does that you may not have recognized as a loving gesture. Equally important to giving to another is receiving what you are given.

_____ 9. Contain who you are; avoid giving too much of yourself away. When you give too much of yourself, you may find yourself adapting and not even notice someone's disrespect (why would someone respect you if you have little regard for yourself?) When this happens, resentment starts to build and loving stops.

In romantic relationships, it is easy to lose self-focus and direct attention too much toward the other person. Be careful not to make him/her your Higher Power. You are more likely to do this if you have experienced some form of abandonment in childhood: emotional (such as criticism or rejection from a parent), spiritual (as in severe physical or sexual abuse or abuse by a spiritual leader), or physical (as in the absence of a parent—even for short periods of time—or physical and sexual abuse). The loss is so great that you may spend much of your adult life seeking that lost attachment—the person who will fill you up, make you feel safe, and give you direction. A most difficult reality adults must face is the realization that no one else can do these things, that we alone must provide this comfort for ourselves. Reparenting the inner child gives a palpable experience of deep love and reduces the need for approval from others. Only then can one enter functional relationships as a whole person.

_____ 10. Take a journey into nature, stand on the rim of the Grand Canyon, or hike to Navajo Arch in Arches National Park; listen to the quiet of the desert or the roar of the ocean;

sit at the base of a giant sequoia or run through the wind rippled grass of a Missouri pasture. Stop, be still and notice what you are given. Stay a little longer just to make sure you have taken it in. Life can get so busy or full that you don't take the time to look around. You will notice that our planet is the greatest act of love any lover could give to a loved one.

_____ 11. Do something ecologically compassionate. Recycle your cans, newspapers, and glass jars. "If all American households recycled newspapers, we could save a million trees every two weeks. If all of us recycled our aluminum cans, we could save enough of the metal to rebuild our entire commercial air fleet every three months." (2) Use fabric shopping bags or reuse the paper or plastic bags you already have. Buy recycled paper products such as toilet paper, paper towels, stationary and cards. Use compact fluorescent light bulbs. "Installing three energy efficient compact fluorescent light bulbs in every home in America could cut forty seven tons of pollution and save six million dollars per day, and eliminate twelve power plants." (3) Use energy-saving shower heads to save 11,400 gallons per person per year. (4) Insulate your homes properly; use double pane windows and wall or ceiling insulation. "Putting thermal shades on our windows could save $26 million a day and eliminate the need for the energy equivalent of fifteen power plants." (4) Turn off the faucet when brushing your teeth or washing dishes. Turn off the lights; turn down the furnace. Layer your clothing and get some exercise (you'll stay warmer). Compost your kitchen scraps. Plant some trees or vegetables. (Share your bounty with a neighbor!) Join a conservation club and give of your money and time. Spend time walking or digging in the dirt so you develop a direct relationship with the earth. Know that you can have a very direct impact on our planet's thriving and imagine how grateful your grandchildren or a friend's grandchildren will be. Planetary consciousness is a profound act of love.

___ 12. Act in love. Love is experienced and expressed in doing. Seek opportunities each day to do loving acts. Love does not miraculously happen to you. Share who you are with another. Express your needs and wants to another person especially when you are unable to meet them for yourself. Show your gratitude and appreciation for your life, even though it is less than satisfying for now. Stay active. Make a point to make your acts of loving visible for now; work on subtlety later. To paraphrase a couple of useful truisms, do what you would have others do for you, for what goes around, comes around.

AFFIRMATIONS FOR EMBRACING LOVE

Choose an affirmation or create one for yourself to repeat daily until you feel it to be true. Alternate two or three throughout the week just to keep it fresh in your awareness. You are not required to believe it before you repeat it to yourself. The goal is to reeducate your brain to recognize truths, not untruths. The miracle of your birth and ability to survive is evidence enough that you are loved and lovable. You have only forgotten this for a short while. Say to yourself:

I am a loving being.
I have the right to be loved and to love others.
I am completely lovable.
In my loving others, I love myself.
In loving others I grow closer to my goal.
I am a gift from God and am perfectly imperfect.
In loving my planet, I love all humankind.
I open myself to true love and recognize when it comes to me.
In giving my partner what s/he wants I am responding in love.
I have a right to love my body and I do.

NOTES

(1) Buscaglia, Leo. *Love*. New York: Fawcett Crest, 1972. p. 98 (Any one of Buscaglia's books are great inspiration for practicing love.

(2) American Forestry Association, **Better Home and Gardens**, April 1991.

(3) Alliance to Save Energy. **Better Home and Gardens**. April, 1991.

(4) Alliance to Save Energy, **Better Homes and Gardens**, April, 1991.

FURTHER READING

1. Goldhor Lerner, *The Dance of Intimacy*, NY: Harper & Row, 1989. This guide for women is for understanding and changing those behaviors which block intimacy.

2. Hendrix. Harville, *Getting the Love You Want*. NY: Harper & Row Publishers, 1988. In my opinion, the best guide available for couples wanting to get closer. Full of writing exercises, as well as tools for understanding why s/he "is just like mom or dad." Includes a good exercise for sharing angry feelings.

3. Vissel, Barry and Joyce. *The Shared Heart*. Aptos. Ca: Ramira Press, 1984. A wonderful guide for relationships and loving.

4. ———, *Models of Love*. A parent's guide to raising loved children. A must for anyone concerned with inner child work, as well.

PAIN

..."*Oh No!*" *sobbed Snaffles,*
"Now water is falling from my eyes."
"That's all right," consoled the rabbit.
Those are only tears. They won't hurt you."
"Tears!" wailed a saddened Snaffles.
"I can't cry. Only babies and sissies cry.
You cheated me rabbit. I wanted to find my emotions and
learn how to laugh and all you gave me was tears."
"No, Snaffles," chuckled the rabbit,
"I didn't cheat you.
You can't find happiness
until you know sadness
and you can't have true laughter
until you know the taste of your own tears.
Look deeper into the water."
Sure enough, Snaffles gazed into the water
and for the first time, saw before him a dirty,
feathery face with tears tracing a dusty line
down his cheeks.
He looked funny,
and the longer he looked
the funnier he looked.
Then from deep, deep inside himself came a
happy rumbling laughter that spilled out
and rolled over the countryside....

Snaffles
by Stephen Cosgrove and Robin James

Chapter 7

PAIN

Emotional pain is the experience of acute discomfort that moves a person to avoid, deny or escape to a more tolerable state of being. Pain hurts, feels bad, is difficult to hold. Human beings will do almost anything to avoid pain.

Grieving involves a processing of pain that takes a person through many different feelings, such as denial, depression anger, shame, hopefulness. Grieving may take a few hours or a few years, depending on the severity of the pain or wound.

Pain results from a loss or abandonment. When a loved one dies or leaves us, when something precious is taken from us, when we are rejected or disrespected, we hurt. Our beliefs or thinking processes magnify and replay an exchange or event. The mind becomes tenacious in its quest to make the loss all right. We search for resolution and acceptance, but if we get stuck here, the mind becomes controlling and can send us into dark places full of self pity, fear and unloving urges.

The natural progression for pain is a welling up from the solar plexus through the throat area to the eyes. As the pain crosses the vocal chords a moan or wail eases the passing. When the pain reaches the eyes, tears flow to wash away the pictures we make and release the ache. Sometimes the pain hurts so deeply there are no tears, only a racking of the body, centered around the heart.

If pain is ignored, left untreated, it begins to fester. When we don't allow the tears or sounds to flow, the wave of anguish arrests. It feels like a lump in the throat, discomfort behind the eyes, headache, or a stone in the pit of the stomach. If we don't share that we are hurt, don't ask for what we need, and continue to get wounded, we start to protect ourselves by building walls or isolating ourselves. Once in the storm of loss, we begin to shut down, hold in, push away. Left in the realm of avoidance, pain becomes chronic and overwhelming. We become depressed, hopeless, and despairing.

When pain flows through us and is expressed, we heal ourselves. As we surrender to the pain, we let go of the loss and eventually find relief in understanding the belief we have held that has kept us in the pain—the "aha!" occurs.

There are many variations of pain:

Disappointment, regret, remorse—that compel us to find new solutions or to make amends to others.

Sadness, sorrow, hurt, heartache—that compel us to weep, sob, moan, wail and seek comfort from other.

Unhappiness, depression, hopelessness—that compel us to "shut down" and marginally function in getting basic needs met.

Agony, grief, anguish, torment misery—that compel us to be alone in the darkness of despair, to curl into a ball, to seek relief in suicidal thinking or addiction.

What goes wrong when we don't feel our pain:
We may
-use anger to bully the pain away
-become chronically depressed
-feel a lack of energy, tired or exhausted, listless, bored.

continued
-be unable to empathize or feel compassion for others
-compensate by using a wall of pleasantness (we are usually quite lonely behind walls)
-use addictive behavior or substances to "feel better"
-make poor decisions
-isolate ourselves
-create safety by not taking risks such as sharing a dream, asking for what we want, or hoping for any thing
-feel chronic self pity

What can go wrong physically when we don't express pain:
-thyroid, goiter, chronic sore throat, inability to swallow
-blindness (not wanting to see reality)
-deafness (not wanting to hear the truth)
-arthritis and other chronic physical pain, aches
-migraine headaches, dizziness, heartburn, shortness of breath
-muscle spasms, back pain
-colitis or constipation
-angina
-cancer (being devoured by our pain)
-crick (in the neck), burning, pangs, soreness
-debilitating diseases resulting from chemical and alcohol abuse
-chronic fatigue syndrome, Epstein Barr virus and other autoimmune diseases
-sleeplessness and loss of appetite
-mental disturbances

TOOLS FOR RECOVERING
AND PRACTICING PAIN

___ 1. Give yourself permission to have your tears. Many children are shamed about crying. They are told to "stop it" or "shut up" because parents can't tolerate the noise or demand. Crying loudly is a wonderful release for pain; crying is the language of pain. I encourage people to embrace pain. I suggest you lean forward, elbows on knees, head down and give sound to the pain. Often people will clench the jaw or stop breathing to keep the pain at bay. Open your mouth, make moaning sounds or "boo-hoo." Remember to breathe, the deeper the better so the body will relax. Tears cleanse the eyes of debris and unwanted pictures and calms the heart. As with all emotions, pain will rise and abate, rise again and abate. Each time, the pain lessens, if only slightly. Sometimes you may need to weep for hours, days, or even months.

The most common complaint I hear from people grieving their lost childhood is that they "should be over the disappointment by now." I believe that the pain will continue to swell until it is released and then you will move on. You may be unable to move beyond the wound because you still see yourself as disempowered, especially if you are offended by a parent figure. Seek a competent therapist who can take you through a cathartic process of addressing the parent you have internalized. Never confront your parents directly, unless they agree to have a therapist or mediator is present. (I have found that this kind of confrontation can require mediation. Some parents are defensive and continue to be abusive. Parents generally did the best they could; they build defenses of denial and minimization to forgive their less than perfect parenting. I have already forgotten the many hours of time and attention I denied my son while we remodeled our home. It hurts too much to hold conscious.)

Writing letters you will never send is another way of expressing the pain and outrage you feel, a way of giving back the shame and pain you hold from the wounding. Judy Tatelbaum says, "It takes enormous courage to face pain directly and honestly, to sit in the midst of such uncomfortable feelings and reactions until we have expressed them and finished with them." (12) Empowerment can also come from making new decisions about how you will take care of yourself in the future.

_____ 2. Write about your pain in a journal. Remember that people tend to overlay feelings on top of feelings. Writing things down helps to sort through the complexities of pain. Generally, the feelings that overlay pain are shame, anger and fear. You may have to begin this exercise by focusing on one of these other emotions to get to the pain. Do not concern yourself with your writing style, punctuation or grammar. Just let the words pour forth, you can make sense of it later if you want. Women, in particular, tend to feel inferior in the area of self expression. Perhaps the first step is to write a letter you won't send to the parent who shamed your intellect or self expression, reclaiming your right to express yourself regardless of any imperfection of style. Then address the following questions:

What am I thinking that is causing this pain?

What am I observing—who did what—and what was my response?

What was my part in it? What did I not say or express?

Where am I hurting in my body?

What can I do to change my response to what happened?

What do I want? What can I say now?

What do I need? (include here things like someone to listen to you, a hug from a friend, time to weep.)

How can I take better care of myself in the future? Make a list of concrete behaviors to draw from. Refrain from making major life decisions here. Good decisions are rarely made during deep grieving—especially those starting with "I will never...."

If you are just beginning to address your pain but you are not sure what it might be about, ask yourself what you feel pain about when others are hurting. In other words we can sometimes feel pain for others but not for ourselves. Write about this.

John James and Frank Cherry suggest several grief exercises in their *Grief Recovery Handbook*. The Loss History Graph is a most useful tool for unraveling the mystery of why a current loss carries the weight of a hundred losses. They suggest making a graph of significant losses since childhood beginning with the first memory. The graph consists of a time/life line divided into quarters. Losses are recorded along this line with a word and the year, with the severity of the losses indicated by the length of the line extending below the time line. What I discovered in doing this exercise is that while I had sustained significant losses in my life, I had wept very little. No wonder I was overwhelmed every time I experienced pain as an adult.

Pia Mellody identifies another significant source of overwhelming pain as the feelings we picked up from our parents when they were out of control with or in denial of their pain. You will know you carry feelings belonging to a parent if you tend toward depression, hopelessness or despair. Her workbook *Breaking Free* is a fine resource for resolving this type of pain.

_____ 3. Claim your right to share your pain, be heard, and receive nurturing. Practice saying these words to at least one other person:

"I am hurting right now. I have a right to hurt. This experience was painful for me and I have a right to tell you about it." Later, add: "And I need you to listen to me, hold me, and support my decision to heal from this." Keep in mind that other people generally have good intentions behind their behavior. When you get hurt by something someone says or does it is your responsibility to let that person know you are hurt, even if it seems most obvious to you. The language and experience of reaching out to another will feel awkward and scary at first, as will receiving the support you have requested. Breathe deeply and say "thank you" as a way of taking in this caring from another.

I believe healing is augmented by sharing with others. Shame is often bound to our various emotions because we were made to feel ashamed about having them. When we speak aloud our feelings, we sever these bonds. Human beings hurt, and weeping is a natural response to hurting. We were not given tears to feel shame each time they flow. Men in particular have struggled with this; culturally, they have been shamed out of their tears. The challenge now is for men to reclaim their right to have and express their pain (shame and fear too). As the atmosphere of acceptance touches each of our lives, our emotional language will become more sophisticated and precise. For now, simply asking for support or offering permission to be sad will do.

_____ 4. Focus on self care. Regardless of whether you are grieving the loss of someone dear to you or the painful memories of childhood, mourning requires a lot of energy. Rest is critical since sleep is often disturbed under conditions of emotional stress. Take naps during the day and reduce some activities such as public service or work if possible. Be sure to eat adequate and nutritious meals (and of course, be careful not to overeat as compensation for filling the hole left by the loss). Addictions flair in response to stress or loss, so be careful to have alternatives. Twelve step meetings and group therapy are very important support options to prevent relapse or self abuse. Maintaining a physical exercise program is important as a way of actively staying out of depression. Exercise releases endorphins (the body's natural opiate)and gives a sense of well being. Make an effort to groom yourself daily. Brushing your hair or teeth, bathing, and even getting dressed may take monumental effort if you are depressed, but you will feel better if you look well. Find a balance between solitude and being with others. There is a danger both of isolating and of filling time with too many social activities. Moderation is the operative word here. Sometimes asking for help to learn what is moderate is useful.

____ 5. Create structure in your life. Grief usually involves a period of disorganization. Besides self care and actively looking at or writing about pain, maintaining a daily routine of activities or goals is important. I have always believed action to be the antidote for depression. Get an appointment book and schedule time for daily grooming activities, meditation or prayer, and journal writing. Notice your environment and choose something daily to improve the quality of your home, yard or community. Perhaps it is new paint for the bedroom or porch, a touch of color in the flower bed, or caring for wounded wild birds. Practice the suggestions given in the chapter on Love. So often we witness in the news people who have turned their tragedy into helpful action. Community service is a terrific way to channel the wounded ego. Pain needs to be directed.

Remember to structure pleasure into your schedule—a visit with a friend, a good movie, a massage, a week on an island beach. You deserve special attention when you are hurting and you are the best person to give to yourself.

____ 6. Find and cultivate your righteous anger. As you will see in the chapter on Anger, anger empowers. Pain is a debilitating emotion. We tend to slow down, regress, or stop moving with pain. Anger provides energy to move and take action. Righteous anger gives us permission to refuse more abuse or hurt, helps to push away and eventually to let go.

List the ways in which the person you are grieving about has hurt you in the past. Note how you felt with each offense. Share this list with someone and give yourself permission to have your feelings about these things. Practice saying "I am hurting about this and I have a right to be angry." This is not an exercise in blaming, but rather a reality check. When a loved one is lost people tend to idolize or create fantasies about that person. Seeing the pain you endured in order to stay connected to someone will help with grieving the loss of what was, as well as the loss of the fantasy. When you find yourself making excuses for the lost one, stop. That human beings do their best and have the best intention is assumed. Your job is to get on with the task of managing and expressing your pain. As you work to complete this task, fill the spaces left from letting go with new and loving thoughts of yourself—"I will choose to honor myself in future relationships," "I am a whole person, complete within myself," "I will survive this loss, grow and greet change with a positive attitude," "I am lovable."

____ 7. Seek understanding and be honest about your pain. What is the lesson you must learn here? Have you been faced with this same lesson in the past? What did you do that prevented you from "getting it" the last time? What is the basic theme of your wounds? What is your responsibility concerning what happened and what will you do to feel better? How does this pain fit with your or God's greater plan for your life? For what are you being honed by lifes painful lessons? How will this pain help you to better serve the world? What is around the corner from change is not always visible. Notice how change has brought you wisdom and opportunity in your life. Even if you don't know for sure why you are having this pain, accept that it may hold a lesson or the motivation toward change, and that you will soon know why.

_____ 8. Always choose life and life supporting behavior. In the darkest moment of deep pain, the mind seeks relief and sometime chooses suicidal thoughts. Suicide must not be an option for dealing with emotional pain. You have the ability to experience the depth of agonizing pain and survive. You may seek to avoid pain because unconsciously you are convinced you will not survive. This may have been true for the child who found many ways to deny or minimize the incredible pain of beatings, abandonment, or sexual abuse. However, as an adult, you now have new tools and skills, wisdom and understanding, vision and faith, and the experience of survival to help manage your pain.

If you are feeling suicidal, find a therapist with whom you feel safe committing to a no suicide contract. Promise that you will call for help when you get these feelings and that if they get strong and tenacious that you will agree to be hospitalized to keep you safe. Select a code word that lets the therapist know you mean business. Otherwise say that you are not serious about the suicide, but you need to share your feelings. Persistent suicidal thinking may become an addictive way of avoiding the discomfort of pain. Having a way out can be comforting, but the consequences eventually become too great.

One of my patients destroyed five cars, got many costly speeding and reckless driving tickets and almost lost her driver's license that would have prevented her from working. She finally found an insurance company to cover her at the price of $5,000 per year. Her suicide addiction kept her quite poor and in constant crisis, but never really out of pain.

_____ 9. Make a new beginning. When you feel you have devoted enough time to pain or grieving, it is time to choose a new direction for your life. This may mean simply doing what you did before with a fresh attitude and hopefulness. Or perhaps you will want to make a career or home move. Maybe just a new coat of fresh paint in your favorite colors will give you a sense of starting over.

Take time to sit with pen and paper to create a new life with healthy decisions. Be impeccably honest with yourself. Sit quietly for a few minutes, breathing deeply. As you settle into yourself, begin to imagine life as you would like it to be. Let all the pictures run through your mind and notice those aspects of your ideal life that require other people to esteem you or fill you up. Now go back through your new life movie and edit those events, replacing them with close-ups of you creating your own esteem and sense of fullness. Be sure to include a commitment to greeting your pain in the future with reverence and gratitude. Know that you feel pain so you will let go and make space for something new to come into your life. Now imagine what this will be and write it down. The last and most important step is to identify, again on paper, what each scene in your movie will require in time and resources—how you will create what you need to get there, and how long you believe it will take for each step. Finally, list the first five things you will do in the next seven days to bring you closer to your goal. Now do these things.

___ 10. Practice forgiveness and acceptance. (See Forgiveness) In the Twelve Step meetings the closing prayer teaches acceptance.

Practice saying:

God, grant me the Serenity to accept the things I cannot change,
the Courage to change the things I can,
and the Wisdom to know the difference.

Then, do your forgiveness work. Work especially to forgive yourself. Let yourself off the proverbial hook. Know that you operated in the best way you knew how, and that you need not continue to hurt yourself or be hurt. Guilt never assuages pain, it only complicates and diverts it. Have compassion for yourself and you will have come a long way in healing your emotional life.

And a woman spoke, saying, Tell us of Pain.
And he said:
Your pain is the breaking of the shell that encloses your understanding.
Even as the stone of the fruit must break, that its heart may stand in the sun, so must you know pain.
And could you keep your heart in wonder at the daily miracles of your life, your pain would not seem less wondrous than your joy;
And you would accept the seasons of your heart, even as you have always accepted the seasons that pass over your fields.
And you would watch with serenity through the winters of your grief.

Much of your pain is self-chosen.
It is the bitter potion by which the physician within you heals your sick self.
Therefore, trust the physician, and drink his remedy in silence and tranquility:
For his hand, though heavy and hard, is guided by the tender hand of the Unseen,
And the cup he brings, though it burns your lips, has been fashioned of the clay which the Potter has moistened with His own sacred tears.

> *Kahlil Gibran*
> *The Prophet*

AFFIRMATIONS FOR EMBRACING PAIN

Affirmations can act more powerfully in your life if you speak them aloud or see them written. Try making banners on your computer or cards in your best calligraphy to post around your home or workspace. Change them periodically so the brain continues to notice them. I always place one above the sink or across from the toilet! In addition to the affirmative statements already suggested in this chapter, practice one of the following daily:

Pain is a gift that teaches me to love and let go.

Pain alerts me to my needs.

Pain reminds me to notice if I am being honest with myself and others.

Through pain I find joy, love and strength.

When I embrace this pain, it will soon pass.

When I have grieved enough, the pain will move to joy.

I will know when it is time to stop grieving.

This pain is helping me to become free.

Pain is the grist, joy the fruit.

I am able to endure and survive the emotional pain I feel.

FURTHER READING

1. Bailey, Linda. *How to Get Going When You Can Barely Get Out of Bed*. NY: Prentice Hall Publishers, 1984. A practical guide for women suffering from depression.

2. Bresler, David E. and Richard Trubo. *Free Yourself From Pain*. New York: Simon & Schuster, 1979.

3. Capacchione, Lucia. *The Creative Journal*. Santa Monica, Ca.: IBS Press, 1988. A wonderful guide into the process of journal writing.

4. ———, *The Well-Being Journal*. Santa Monica, Ca.: IBS Press, 1989. A guide for using your writing to heal yourself.

5. James, John; Cherry, Frank; *The Grief Recovery Handbook*. New York: Harper & Row Publishers, 1988. I am recommending this handbook to many of my clients because of its useful suggestions for grief recovery. I especially like the strong suggestion to do this work with another person.

6. Kubler-Ross, Elizabeth. *On Death an Dying*. New York: Macmillan, 1969. The grandparent of books on understanding the grief process.

7. ———, *Death: The Final Stage of Growth*. Englewood Cliffs, NJ: Prentice-Hall, 1975.

8. Kuhner, Harold S. *When Bad Things Happen to Good People*. New York: Schocken, 1981; New York Avon, 1983.

9. Progoff, Ira. *At a Journal Workshop: The Basic Guide and Text for Using the Intensive Journal*. New York: Dialogue House Library. 80 E. 11th St., New York 1981. A great resource for guiding writing journal .

10. Roth, Deborah. *Stepping Stones to Grief Recovery*. Santa Monica, Ca.: IBS Press. 1989. Offers practical help for those facing the loss of someone close.

11. Staudacher, Carol, *Beyond Grief*. Santa Monica, Ca.: IBS Press. 1989. Offers a step by step approach to recovery.

12. Tatelbaum. Judy, *The Courage to Grieve*. New York: Harper & Row Publisher, 1980. An excellent reference for people seeking a model for grieving. Ms. Tatelbaum offers useful tools for working through loss and pain. I highly recommend this resource.

ANGER

...Anastasia was very quiet for a moment.
She was thinking about what the Queen Mother had said.

"Queen Mother, when I was angry and grumpy,
so was everybody else around me.
Everybody except you, that is.
Why were you never angry and grumpy with me, Queen Mother?"

"My child, my child, I always saw your Higher Self whenever I looked at
you!
When I saw the very best that is in you
every time I looked at you,
how could I possibly be angry and grumpy with you?"

Anastasia reached out and hugged her grandmother
in a great bear hug.
She planted a warm kiss on her beautiful cheek....

The Magic Mirror
by Linda Moffit

Chapter 8

ANGER

Anger is generally confused with rage. Men particularly have been groomed in our culture to rage and intimidate, in the guise of machismo or manliness. Anger is actually a more centered, empowering experience. Rage feels scary, overwhelming, out of control, violent destructive and even lethal. Rage turned inward becomes extremely dangerous, wreaking havoc on self esteem, spirituality, and the ability to be intimate with others. Rage feels awful.

Anger is the experience of intense energy that flows through the body, generally stimulating the release of adrenaline, that compels a person to protect or defend. The stimulus for anger is often a threat to the physical body or to the emotional, spiritual, or intellectual well being of a person. We may feel misjudged or misunderstood and seek justice to exonerate ourselves. Anger helps us to feel more powerful, gives us the strength to do what we must do to protect ourselves or loved ones, and empowers us to set limits with others when they offend us. No one gets hurt when anger is expressed appropriately.

One reason for the confusion between anger and rage is that people don't moderate anger very well. They withhold their feelings of pain, disappointment, shame or anger until something, like the straw and the camel's back, triggers an explosion. In addition, many have had anger modeled as rage or withholding, leading to uncontrolled outbursts or resentments.

Anger is often repressed or withheld, misdirected or projected onto others. The pushy, obnoxious kid in school or the father who threatens his children use bullying to express their shame or fear. The mother martyrs herself for her children, changing to saccharine sweetness her resentment over lack of time alone or a hot meal. The list keeper, who never lets go of anyone's wrong doing, repeatedly brings up mistakes or offenses. The husband or wife who is always tired rarely has enough energy for affection, sharing or sex. The life of the party who always has a joke, even if it isn't funny, will talk about his wife with sarcasm and ridicule. Anger in these forms causes emotional damage to self and others.

Some children rarely experience anger without being hurt or seeing someone else hurt. Others never see anger expressed at all. Unfortunately, this means that when we do see appropriate anger in others, we may have a tendency to be frightened or expect the worst. When this happens we find ourselves on the cycle of defending and attacking, being aggressive and withholding, anger begetting anger.

Anger, in its extreme, rises from the solar plexus, gathers intensity, fills the chest and shoulders, and rushes out the arms compelling the hands to make fists to strike. Sometimes the anger pulses down through the large muscle of the legs giving strength and power to run or chase. Because anger is so much an action emotion, we tend to use it to counter the immobilizing effects of pain, fear or shame.

Once anger reaches a certain intensity, intervention becomes increasingly difficult. Up to a certain point, we remain rational and able to make reasonable requests, reconnect, forgive. However, unless we do something to calm ourselves, we will tend to think more irrationally (in black and white, either/or); we will lose ourselves in a rage or behind a wall of silence. Once out of control, the return to rationality becomes arduous, time consuming and lonely. Early intervention, anger reduction work and lots of practice at being assertive are the most effective tools for staying centered through anger.

There are many variations of anger:

Annoyance, displeasure, vexation—probably the mildest forms of anger; feels bothersome like gnats, mosquitoes and broken things.

Exasperation, perturbation, petulance, irritation, indignation, peevishness—more urgent quality of anger compelling one to say something, set limits or act to correct the situation.

Agitation, outrage, provocation, animosity, ire, wrath, fury, hostility—more extreme forms of anger that may push us to rage, loudly express ourselves, or hurt ourselves or others.

What goes wrong when we don't feel our anger:
We may:
-wall ourselves off from others, making ourselves unapproachable.
-rant and rave, throw things, hurt our children or those closest to us.
-look or act helpless or powerless
-be victimized by others
-offend others, especially our children, by exploding or seething, passively hurting them through neglect or deliberate meanness
-lack assertiveness or the ability to speak or defend
-resent and withhold
-armor ourselves with pleasantness
-be unclear in requests and angry when we don't get what we want
-martyr ourselves
-land in jail from a rage attack
-attempt suicide from self hate

What can go wrong physically when we don't express our anger:
-chronic jaw, neck or back pain
-tooth pain or abrasion from grinding or clenching
-TMJ (temporomandibular joint), grinding, headaches, earaches
-hypertension, high blood pressure
-heart attack
-disc degeneration
-colon, rectal cancer
-colitis, diarrhea, constipation
-weight retention
-kidney, gall bladder, liver problems
-arthritis

TOOLS FOR RECOVERING
AND PRACTICING ANGER

_____ 1. Begin by noticing what you find annoying or mildly irritating, either in the past or present. Write these down. Notice how you did or did not react at the time. Notice how long or under what circumstances it took for you to react. Get an idea of how you process around this emotion. Notice what causes you righteous indignation when things happen to others. Note if these things have ever happened to you. Answer the following questions:

-Do I stuff anger? How?
-Do I throw things? Break things?
-Do I retreat and hold resentment?
-Do I rage at or blame others?
-Do I blame myself?
-Do I get sick or hurt myself?

-What do I share? What do I withhold?

-Under what circumstances do I do each?

If you find that you are angry with yourself much of the time, remember that we humans are imperfect so we can learn and grow. There are no rules that say a human being must be perfect despite what you heard from an overly demanding or perfectionistic parent. People make mistakes all the time. Forgive yourself by declaring your right to make mistakes and own that you always do the best you can under the circumstances.

_____ 2. Write about or share with someone how anger has been modeled for you throughout your life. Be sure to include heroes from television, movies, and books that were significant to you. Look specifically at each of your caregivers as you were growing up and how they did or did not express anger. Record how you felt when anger was directed toward you. Now, share how you behave when you get angry. We often marry or are attracted to partners who model the same or opposite behavioral extreme of anger. How does your spouse manifest either extreme? Be honest in your assessment. You will heal yourself and avoid offending others in the future.

_____ 3. Become aware of when you use anger to mask another emotion. Harville Hendrix, in *Getting the Love You Want*, describes a "container" exercise that allows time for a person to feel heard, be validated and express the deepest levels of pain, fear or shame disguised as anger. This seven step process involves asking a partner to "contain" his/her anger or responses while you share your annoyance, irritation or ire. Whenever I have seen this demonstrated or practiced it myself, I have found that there has usually been another, more vulnerable feeling underlying the anger. Remember that anger empowers us to let others know we are being offended so we can be safe, included and more connected.

Because anger has been hurtful in some of our experiences,

we tend to defend or attack when someone confronts us. Or we may be so frightened of confronting that we may attack or defend first.

Feeling safe with another person is necessary before we can feel free to share our more vulnerable feelings. When we can do this, more meaningful and healing communication occurs.

When you must confront someone, act from a place of caring, respect and love. Assume that the person who has offended you does not know he has offended you and accept that it is your job to let him know. People do not generally offend out of spite or meanness. More often, they offend out of ignorance and omission, narcissism and selfishness.

____ 4. Act responsibly with your anger. Follow these rules for your safety and the safety of others.

- **You have a right to your anger, others have a right to theirs**
- **You must not hurt anyone**
- **You must not hurt yourself**
- **You must not destroy anything**

Many people are terrified of their own anger. As with pain, they believe that "if I allow myself to feel any anger, I will die or hurt someone and they will die." The truth is that someone probably did get hurt when anger was expressed in their families. Someone screamed at or hit them, beat mom or left dad because he wasn't an adequate provider.

Over the years of working with childhood wounds, I so often hear that people would rather stuff anger, work it away, or die than express it to another person. Our early conditioning is very powerful. But we need anger, it is an ally and a friend. And so we must become comfortable with its presence in the body and its expression in relationship. People who do not express anger are very difficult to live with. We never know where we stand with them. We experience covert, sneaky aggression from that person rather than direct clear information. This keeps us dancing and dodging, and always failing.

_____ 5. Be grateful for your anger. With all the emphasis on spirituality and forgiveness, it is easy to circumvent anger by "spiritualizing" it away. To be "good," children accept from parents that being angry is wrong or hurtful. They are made to feel guilty, told to "turn the other cheek," and to not be bothered by what another child does to them. Children are told to "be quiet" or "be good" when they go crying to mom or dad. Some religions promote ideas of fellowship or compassion that can be misunderstood to mean "don't ever be angry or show it if you are."

We grow to believe we are bad if we are angry or we will loose our place in heaven if we express our anger. Sometimes God's punishment is used as a threat to control our angry outbursts.

We must come to terms with whatever has made us angry. However, the reason for this is not to be more spiritually acceptable, but to be free of the burden of holding resentment or disappointment. Forgiveness and acceptance help us to let go so we can move on to new opportunities and connections with others. Your anger must be moderated and expressed in non-hurtful ways, but it is purposeful and useful, and god-given.

_____ 6. Inventory your anger. Take a piece of paper and divide it into five columns. At the top of each column, write the following headings: **I am angry about...And I'd like to tell...And I would say...What I really feel is...What I can do about it is....** Now begin to list each of your peeves. Then go back and answer the second column and so on. When you get to the last column, be as specific as you can and clear about what you would be willing to do.

Your finished product ought to read something like this: **I am angry about** my husband's lack of communication with me...**And I'd like to tell** him...**And I would say** "I feel lonely when you don't share who you are with me, I don't feel safe to be sexual with you when we haven't shared much verbally, and I want a partner who is present"...**What I really feel** is sad, lonely, left out and hurt...**What I can do about this is** tell him how I feel, ask for what I want, be vulnerable and share who I am more, ask for us to see a counselor, make a decision to leave him, or be grateful for what I have and let it go.

Much of what we upset ourselves over is a perceived lack of options. Feelings of powerlessness can insight fury in an instant. This exercise reminds us that we always have choices.

_____ 7. Use good boundaries when expressing anger. Boundaries help in remembering those rules in number four above. Whenever someone confronts you with anger, your job is to shield yourself for protection, listen quietly and relay back what you heard that person say. Standing too close to someone you are confronting or who is confronting you can cause you to be confused. Move yourself a few feet away. When confronting, watch for non-verbal cues that indicate you are too close. Those cues may include the other person's inability to maintain eye contact, a tilted head, body leaning back and away, or verbal confusion. Boundaries increase the chances for clear communication and understanding.

With anger, we tend to break rules of verbal etiquette, saying what we would never say in other circumstances. We also may offend by threatening with tone and volume of voice, body posturing or fists and facial expression. Screaming, hitting, pushing or pulling, forcing sexual activity and throwing things at another person are serious boundary violations. We are responsible for making amends when we do these things and for making a commitment not to do them again. However, when we offend in other ways, it is the victim's responsibility to let us know of the offense. Remember that most people have a positive intention behind what they say and do, even in anger. Generally they want to be connected and to feel loved or respected. I have found people to be most willing to apologize when they have offended, especially when their positive intention is acknowledged.

_____ 8. Express your anger. Anger compels you to act. For reducing long term anger, also for an immediate release, practice any of the following several times a week.

Use your voice to release held energy by finding a safe and alone place to scream, growl, or yell (I use my car with the windows rolled up or sometimes I go into the forest). If you cannot get away, scream into a pillow or a towel.

Throw something: rocks into a body of water or at old glass bottles you don't care about (and then sweep them up and take them to be recycled).

Wring a towel.

Use boxing gloves to punch a hanging bag of sawdust.

Use a plastic or foam bat (bataca) to hit a bed.

Find a partner and push each other with pillows.

Represent your anger in a collage, with paint or pencil, or in three dimensional form. Visualize the anger in or out of your body. See what it looks like when it explodes. See how you stop it before it explodes. Give it color, shape, size, texture, proportion, brightness or darkness, taste or sound. Represent what it covers up and how. Keep an anger portfolio and watch how it changes over time.

Write a poem or story or journal entry about your anger. Write a dialogue with the anger and ask its intention. Ask for its help to get you what you really want. Ask what it needs in order to cooperate with you. Write a letter you won't send to the person who has offended you. Commit to following through on setting limits or expressing yourself directly to another person.

Do some kind of aerobic physical activity such as running, jogging, bicycling, swimming, or dancing.

Repeat to yourself internally or aloud "I am angry and I have a right to be angry!"

___ 9. Take a Time Out if you feel like you might rage. Count to fifty, take a walk, go to your room, breathe deeply, ask for ten minutes of silence while you compose yourself. If you leave let the other person know when you will return and follow through. If you find you are still not ready to talk, ask for another fifteen minutes. Avoid any behavior that will medicate your anger such as drinking alcohol or caffeine, smoking, eating, demanding sex, driving too fast, etc. The goal is not to become numb, but to be present enough to express what you feel or need by distancing yourself either spatially or temporally until you become calm. This is probably the most important skill you can learn for containing and expressing your anger. Offending others does not get us what we want and usually only brings on more dire consequences.

___ 10. Use the following format to express anger appropriately:

-Know what you feel under the anger by doing the above exercises. Validate your right to feel and share what you feel.

-Diffuse the anger by using the suggestions in numbers 8 & 9 or discuss it with a therapist or friend first.

-Tell your partner you need to express your anger about something.

-Ask when it will be convenient to talk and wait if it is not convenient now. Agree to a length of time for the sharing.

-Set your boundaries and face each other.

-Use John Bradshaw's Awareness Wheel and do not deviate (the person listening does not defend or explain):

   -What I heard you say was....

   -What I saw you do was....

-My interpretation was....

-My feelings are (use words like hurt, afraid, embarrassed)....

-What I want is....

-The listener now feeds back what was said and offers empathic support like "That must have felt awful."

-Take a break and give the listener time to collect thoughts

-Now reverse roles.

-If you have offended someone, even unknowingly, you must make amends or at the very least, agree to a time when you will be ready to do so. Asking for and giving forgiveness is very important for getting completion. Holding on will only build resentments and keep you stuck in darkness. Each partner must be willing to fulfill the requests made or at least indicate what s/he needs in order to do so. Harville Hendrix recommends doing something playful or aerobic to complete the exercise. I have found a hug can give a feeling of closure.

AFFIRMATIONS FOR EMBRACING ANGER

Many times, people need permission to be angry because experience has shown anger to be hurtful. These affirmations will help to affirm your right to have healthy anger. Practice these affirmations by saying them aloud or to another person.

I have a right to my anger.

My anger empowers and strengthens me.

I have a right to express my anger.

I can express my anger in a way that is physically safe for myself and others.

If I am appropriate with my anger, everyone will be safe.

My righteous anger lets others know where I stand.

I gain another's respect when I set limits.

My higher power loves me when I am angry too.

When I express my anger appropriately, I take care of
myself.
My responsibility is to let others know when they have
hurt me.

FURTHER READING

1. Goldhor Lerner, Harriet, *The Dance of Anger*. New York,
Harper & Row, 1985. An especially important guide for
women in relationships.

2. Hendrix, Harville, *Getting the Love You Want*. New
York: Harper & Row, 1988.

3. McKay, Matthew; Rogers, Peter; and McKay, Judith,
When Anger Hurts. Oakland, Ca.: New Harbinger Publications, Inc., 1989. An excellent guide for understanding how
anger develops. Especially helpful for people who tend to lash
out.

4. Rubin, Theodore Isaac, *The Angry Book*. New York:
Macmillan Publishing Co., 1969. A terrific book, has been
around a long time and is still timely and relevant. One of the
best.

FEAR

...They thought that was only the modesty becoming to a hero,
and before they would believe him he had to explain
how the Monster had only seemed big
so long as he was running away, and that
the nearer he got to it the smaller it grew,
until at last, when he was standing beside it,
he could pick it up in his hand.

The people crowded around to see the Monster.
It woke up, yawned a small puff of smoke,
and began to purr.
A little girl asked Miobi. "What is its name?"
"I don't know," said Miobi. "I never asked it."
The Monster itself answered her question.
It stopped purring, looked around
to make sure everyone was listening,
and then said:
"I have many names. Some call me Famine, and some Pestilence;
but the most pitiable humans give me their own names."
It yawned again, and then added,
"But most people call me What-Might-Happen."

> *The Monster That Grew Small*
> *by Joan Grant*

Chapter 9

FEAR

Fear must be distinguished from anxiety, phobias, and panic attacks. Functional fear acts as an alarm clock, calls us to pay attention, look around and protect ourselves from potential dangers. Fear motivates us to act, to get ourselves to a safe place, or to defend against injustice. Fear is induced by a specific and concrete stimulus. Anxiety, on the other hand, is more generalized.

Phobias are overwhelming fears of such things as elevators, sickness or germs, crowded places, public bathrooms or heights. Phobias produce involuntary physiological responses that interfere with our ability to work, get ourselves around, or perform at work or home. Phobias are healed through desensitization and visualization, education and practice.

A panic attack seems to come from nowhere, is intensely uncomfortable (as with the terror of impending death), and may be a single wave of feeling or may recur in waves for several hours. Panic attacks can occur after a recent loss, such as death or separation, triggering the feeling of abandonment or aloneness. Inner child work can be of tremendous benefit in these instances as the root of the fear usually resides in childhood. Sometimes medication is used to interrupt the attacks until a person can get his/her bearings and begin the adjustment process. Other causes of panic attacks may include a major life change, such as a move or illness, initial or extensive use of caffeine or cocaine, hypoglycemia, PMS, hyperventilation, hyperthyroidism or heart palpitations. Fear of panic attacks can contribute to a general feeling of anxiety.

With intense fear, the body responds with a rush of adrenaline, shortness of breath, racing heart, flushing, a sense of urgency to flee or fight, narrowing of peripheral vision, throbbing in the head, ringing in the ears, sweaty palms trembling, cold in the extremities, and/or an inability to move at all.

In contrast to phobic responses and panic attacks, healthy fear feels moderately uncomfortable in the chest, middle of the back, solar plexus and chest. There may be some of the above physiology present but it will tend to be in a milder form, pass more quickly and may feel less intense. Certainly, a pit bull threatening your throat will elicit a sense of urgency, allowing you to call for help or flee. For those of us who have lived with fear much of our lives, fear is experienced as a "sense" that something is awry. We have developed an intuition about our surroundings that we have grown to trust. Over time, we become wise to potential dangers and act instinctively in situations, such as when crossing the street we look both ways or when children are around, we stay alert to their proximity to the stove.

Fear is most often disguised by anger or rage, especially in men. The fear/rage response is so immediate that it often takes much sorting to get to the awareness of the underlying fear, which is usually about safety (fear of death or being hurt), loss (fear of abandonment or being destitute), or pride (fear of being seen as stupid, less than or incapable). Other common masks for fear are an overuse of humor, incessant talking, bravado, "machismo" or fearlessness. As a chronic state, fear may keep us from asserting ourselves, protecting our children, or leaving unhealthy situations. We may also bully people, terrorize our children, or aggressively insist on our own way.

The following are some variations:

Awe, reverence—often in response to something incomprehensible, threatening or overpowering.

Dread, apprehension, worry, trepidation—give a sense of discomfort, something is not quite right.

Mistrust, distrust, suspicion—awareness of incongruities or inconsistency especially in another person.

Hypervigilance, anxiousness, nervousness—indicate disturbance and acute alertness to outside stimuli.

Dismay, horror, terror—responses to atrocity or extreme danger.

What goes wrong when we don't feel our fear:
We may:
-find ourselves in dangerous situations because we
 have missed the cues
-have an over-inflated bravado
-get very busy in order to avoid people or situations
-smoke cigarettes
-practice addictive behavior
-approach/avoid people, situations, or success
-have a high pitched voice indicating shallow breathing
-be overly concerned, preoccupied, with our children's
 safety, giving messages that the world is not safe
-push people away rather than be rejected
-isolate, become phobic or obsessive/compulsive
-dissociate from our bodies, go numb
-shout or scream a lot
-have nightmares
-be unable to talk in front of others
-become hypersensitive to others
-lack a clear sense of self

What can go wrong physically when we don't express fear:
-asthma, hyperventilation, breathing disorders
-allergies
-colon problems: colitis, bowel obstruction, cancer,
-candida
-autoimmune disease
-addictions (work, sex, love, tobacco, exercise, danger, etc)
-frequent accidents, broken bones, bruises, scrapes, burns
-ulcers, gastritis, stomach pain, digestive problems
-palpitations and heart attack
-back and shoulder pain
-nervous disorders, tics

TOOLS FOR RECOVERING
AND PRACTICING FEAR

_____ 1. Assess the nature and frequency of your fearless behavior. Sometimes in your urgency to avoid feeling out of control, powerless and frightened, you may swing to the opposite extreme of having no fear at all. In doing this, you deflect fear to others and may act without conscience or healthy caution. In your journal, write about the following questions:
-how have I frightened others in my life?
-do I speed, do I take chances on the road?
-how many car accidents have I had?
-does my recreational activities involve adrenaline
   highs (such as hang gliding, parachuting, bungy
   jumping, white water rafting, ocean kayaking, etc.)?

-who have I threatened and how?

-how have I endangered myself or others (hanging out of windows, walking on the outside of bridges, gone as far out on a cliff as possible, stood on the edge of a fiery volcano, operated machinery while intoxicated, not used seat belts, etc.)?

-have I agitated wild animals, taken risks of being mauled?

-are my children frequently hurt because of my inattentiveness?

-do I lose pets or endanger them?

-do I wait until the last minute to do important things

-do I engage in illegal activities with the likelihood of getting caught?

-do I use cigarettes, drugs or alcohol to calm myself?

____2. Get clear about what is dangerous. Because of a lack of supervision in childhood, severe handling or a parent's drug or alcohol abuse, many people have little or no sense of what is safe and what is dangerous. We have been desensitized to our own fear cues and no longer recognize them. Frances, victim of a prior rape and battering, walked to the river one day, passing a man who was masturbating just off the path. Rather than retreat to the safety of her car, she continued deeper into the brush where she had no way out when he pursued her. When I questioned her about her thinking, she revealed that it had occurred to her that he might be dangerous but he didn't "look" like he would hurt her and she wanted to get to the river.

When you have no internal way of assessing danger, you must educate yourself by asking or observing others. Find out what is scary to others, what they think about walking at night or what kind of people they consider unsafe. Start to notice potential problems in your surrounding, such as children playing on the sidewalk with a ball, a cyclist riding too close to parked cars, a man in the shadows as you walk to your car.

As you imagine what might go wrong, notice how you feel in your body and where you feel it. The goal here is not to create paranoia and panic, but to lead you into an awareness of your body's sense of alertness.

When in doubt, lean toward caution. It is reasonable that a convicted child molester will make a poor parent for your children, that your chances for severe head injury increase when you don't wear your motorcycle helmet, or that walking down the middle of the street is best if you must walk at night in the city. Do whatever it takes to get safe. Don't put yourself in an unwholesome situation; your job is to build trust and a sense of security within yourself. Educate your biological children about safety, because you care about them. As with any new behavior, use moderation in sensitizing yourself to danger. The world doesn't have to be a scary place, you just need to be able to hear your inner alarm clock when there is a real danger and find safety.

_____ 3. Become adept at seeing your own fear. Reliable indicators of fear are the tendency to avoid situations or people and resistance to trying new behaviors. Notice if you do any of the following:

-isolate yourself
-make frequent relationship changes
-fail at a job or task, when you are well equipped to succeed
-refuse to ask for help
-talk little or too much
-pursue others only when they retreat, flee when you are pursued
-teach your children the world is not safe
-procrastinate
-lie or withhold the truth
-clam up when it comes to asking for what you want or need

-worry a lot, imagine disasters
-scream when the situation calls for calm
-put others down, criticize or minimize their accomplishments

This list is just to prompt recognition of your fears and how you behave around them. Give yourself permission to begin to change some of these behaviors, in small steps. Finding the root trauma or problem is useful, but not necessary, and is material for work with a competent therapist. Meantime, you can begin to make small changes by practicing these suggestions. As you make behavioral changes your confidence will build.

_____ 4. Identify and address defense mechanisms that no longer support you. Although fear is an ally that helps you to survive, sometimes it gets in the way when you need or want to grow or change. While these defenses help to survive childhood, they can prohibit intimate connection with others or successful accomplishments.

Do the following exercise in your journal or in your imagination.

-Center yourself, breathe deeply. Open your mind to
 discovery and your heart to freedom. Be welcoming.
-Ask your fear to show itself to you. Listen and watch what
 comes up. Don't censor or analyze.
-Give your fear form, texture, shape, smell, sound.
-Ask its purpose or goal. Keep asking until you learn the
 positive intention. Thank the fear for keeping you safe.
-Ask fear what it needs to let you move on in your life.
 Listen carefully.
-Let fear know how you intend to protect and take care of
 yourself in the future. Assure fear that you will keep the
 part of fear that helps you to pay attention to potential
 danger.
-Identify what feeling you want to replace the fear with

(such as confidence, being centered, acceptance) and ask the fear if it would be willing to share space with this new feeling. If not, ask what it needs in order to do so. Make a commitment to do what it requests. Then ask again for its cooperation.

-Now look again at the fear. Watch it get smaller and farther away. See it change color and get dimmer. Put it in a container or a place in your body where you feel you can manage it. Or set it in the desert surrounded by cactus thorns.

-Now see yourself acting in the future with your new emotion, fulfilling your intended behavior, safe, with the awareness that your fear will alert you to real danger.

-Take some deep breaths and center yourself in your new confidence.

____ 5. Educate and empower yourself further. Take advantage of class offerings in assertiveness training, drivers training, public speaking, martial arts, or model mugging. Participate in a support or therapy group to gain confidence in expressing and sharing yourself. Learn a new skill related to your fears, such as meditation when you are afraid to be alone, star gazing when you are afraid of the dark, or money management when you are afraid of being destitute.

As you move toward your fear with determination and faith that you will overcome it, your fear will become less threatening or debilitating. This may take some time, but be tenacious. I spent ten years visiting snakes in zoos, aquariums, and pet stores, asking to touch, stroke and eventually hold them, reading books about safe and poisonous kinds (and where they live). I even imagined being a snake. Now I can comfortably come upon one in the garden. I even feel a tenderness for and appreciation of them. If you cannot imagine yourself healing a phobia alone, find a therapist who can help desensitize you.

_____ 6. Get comfortable with your voice. With fear a natural tendency of the body is to shut down (or up, as the case may be). Singing requires you to breathe deeply, causing the body to relax. Also, it opens up the throat, jaw, and lungs, releasing any holding you might be doing. Singing stretches and tones the vocal chords and encourages the voice to take on tone, depth and resonance. The speaking voice becomes more powerful. Sometimes women speak with a voice that is either too high pitched or too soft to be taken seriously. Men tend to be loud or intimidating with their voices. Power can be felt by lowering the voice into the chest and utilizing the breath more evenly. A simple yet forcefully resonating "No!" can be enough to deter a potential offender.

When you have difficulty speaking aloud, practice reading aloud, reciting poetry, or humming when you are alone. Teach someone, a child perhaps, how to do a task or skill. Work your way to hooting, hollering, shouting, or screaming in the forest or at a baseball game. Emitting sound when you are frightened is very important for the disbursement of adrenaline and the releasing of the breath. Fear's energy needs to go somewhere. Sound is empowering and harmless to others, unless of course you are shouting in someone's face. Then it becomes quite harmful.

Practice the words "I am frightened right now. I have a right to be frightened. Will you reassure me, hold me or stay close to me?"

_____ 7. Strengthen yourself physically. Having a sense of your own strength and coordination helps you to be able to protect yourself or your loved ones. If you are a small person, adding muscle and speed offers a sense of empowerment. Martial arts teaches skills in defending, centeredness under stress, and use of your voice to release tension and give strength to your action. Even if you never use a hold or kick, having the physical awareness will increase confidence.

Exercise can take many forms—lifting weights, aerobics, running, calinetics©, rowing or yoga. Work for strength, tone, muscle mass, and coordination. Even if you never have to defend yourself, you will feel terrific.

_____ 8. Live in the present. Gerald Jampolsky in *Love is Letting Go of Fear* teaches us to look for love in all things, to let go of past hurts or disappointments, and to focus attention on the perfection of the present moment. Whenever you move out of the here and now, you enter the realm of anticipation, anxiety, and fear. Understanding that how you choose to see the moment will determine your experience can lead to a great sense of empowerment. I can see my last ten dollars as the beginning of hell on earth or an adventure in self care. I can also see it as an opportunity to trust my inner resources to create what I need. I can trust in my Higher Power to keep me safe, comfortable and loved.

One of my closest friends was living in a community where, in exchange for extensive therapy, training, a room, and food, she had to work a few hours a day in the kitchen. When she visited one day she complained of how frightened she was of not having a car, a job, a house and money to buy things. I asked her what frightened her about that and she said she didn't want to become destitute. When I reminded her that she was already destitute because she didn't have these things and that she was living quite comfortably, we had a good laugh. She had simply neglected to notice that she was already doing the very thing she feared the most and it wasn't all that bad!

_____ 9. Tell someone else about your fear. Sometimes just saying it aloud will dissipate its power. If you tend to shame yourself about being afraid, telling someone will help to show that you are most likely not alone in your fear. A client recently told me she got enough courage to tell her best friend that she is terrified of bugs, physical ailments and things falling from the sky. Her friend hooted with relief because she thought she was the only one who was so "silly." Now they tease each other, lovingly, about bugs and Chicken Little. They are sharing the task of lightening the load and expressing their fears openly.

_____ 10. Seek the ultimate source of your safety. Remember that you are here by design. Your physical form and the power of your thinking demonstrates purpose and meaning. The gift of our exquisite planet is the greatest proof that you are loved. No creator of such beauty and vulnerability could abandon its creation without a promise of regeneration or protection.

Imagine a loving source of divine guidance, affirming every life supporting act you do, urging you on to higher levels of functioning, loving you as you fall, and giving infinite life to your very soul. Your physical form is the clothing you must wear to evolve your soul as you walk the earth. God's love is the cloak that carries your soul home and sends you back when it is time to grow again. Look homeward for understanding and meaning, and entrust your care and guidance to your Creator.

AFFIRMATIONS FOR EMBRACING FEAR

Affirmations can be powerful tools in the healing of fear. Safety is the key to the successful management of your fear. Be assured that you have a right to do whatever it takes to be safe. Practice these affirmations:

My safety is more important than another's feelings.
I have a right to protect myself by removing myself from a dangerous situation.
Fear is my friend and ally.
Fear protects me and keeps me safe.

When my body trembles and shakes, I am probably feeling frightened.

I notice danger cues such as darkness, screaming, hitting, fast driving, sneaky behavior, etc.

I have a right to protect my child from danger, even if it means saying "No."

I trust God or my Higher Power to take care of me.

I become more human and more whole as I express my fear.

FURTHER READING

1. Burns David. *Feeling Good.* NY Signet 1981. Good reading on cognitive distortions.

2. Bourne, Edmund J., *The Anxiety & Phobia Workbook.* Oakland. Ca: New Harbinger Publications. Inc. 1990. The definitive book on self help for anxiety and phobias, also for managing most emotions.

3. Handly, Robert and Neff, Pauline. *Anxiety and Panic Attacks: Their Cause and Cure.* NY: Rawson Associates, 1985. Useful affirmations and visualizations for phobias.

4. Hunt, Douglas. *No More Fears.* NY Warner Books, 1988.

5. Jampolsky, Gerald, *Love is Letting Go of Fear.* Millbrae, Ca: Celestial Arts, 1979. A classic in the literature on changing thinking to change emotions and herald for *A Course in Miracles*.

6. *A Course in Miracles*. NY Foundation for Inner Peace, 1975. A very useful step by step guide for correcting limited thinking leading the student to a higher level of thinking and functioning in the world and spiritually.

SHAME

...*"Now look here, Toad,"* said the Rat.

"It's about this Banquet, and very sorry I am to have to speak to you like this. But we want you to understand clearly, once and for all, that there are going to be no speeches and no songs. Try and grasp the fact that on this occasion we're not arguing with you; we're just telling you."

Toad saw that he was trapped. They understood him, they saw through him, they had got ahead of him.

His pleasant dream was shattered.

"Might I sing them just one little song?" he pleaded piteously.

"No, not one little song," replied the Rat firmly, though his heart bled as he noticed the trembling lip of the poor disappointed Toad.

"It's no good, Toady, you know well that your songs are all conceit and boasting and vanity, and your speeches are all self praise and—and—well, and gross exaggeration and—and ..."

"And gas," put in the Badger, in his common way.

"It's for your own good, Toady," went on the Rat.

"You know you must turn over a new leaf sooner or later, and now seems a splendid time to begin; a sort of turning point in your career. Please don't think that saying all this doesn't hurt me more than it hurts you."

Toad remained a long while plunged in thought.

At last he raised his head, and the traces of strong emotion were visible on his features.

"You have conquered, my friends," he said in broken accents.

"It was, to be sure, but a small thing that I asked—merely leave to blossom and expand for yet one more evening, to let myself go and hear the tumultuous applause that always seems to me—somehow— to bring out my best qualities.

However, you are right, I know, and I am wrong.

Henceforth I will be a very different Toad.

My friends, you shall never have occasion to blush for me again.

But, O dear, O dear, this is a hard world!"

The Wind in the Willows
by Kenneth Grahame

Chapter 10

SHAME and GUILT

Although shame and guilt are sometimes used inter-changeably, a distinction must be made between them. Shame is the emotion we feel when we become aware of our limitations. We feel embarrassed when we make a social mistake, are reminded by someone else of our failings, don't live up to our own expectations or the expectation of others, or have caused others distress. Shame also carries a sense of humility which inspires us to look to a Higher Power for comfort, help, or gratitude for the gifts of our lives. Shame is a very evolved emotion, designed to keep us in contact with deeper values that stem from awareness of a power much greater than ourselves. Healthy shame moves us from our humanness to our divine origin and purpose. We are reminded who we are. We need shame to keep us equal so we will act respectfully toward ourselves and others.

Healthy guilt similarly keeps us acting responsibly toward others but has more to do with rules and values than acceptance and approval. When we break with our own sense of integrity by acting contrary to a value we hold, we become disturbed by our behavior and feel compelled to correct the situation. Guilt motivates us to act with a sense of duty, honesty, and principle.

These healthy emotions turn to unhealthy shame or guilt when children get condemning messages from adults or peers like being imperfect is bad, the child's mere existence is intolerable, or the child is responsible for the parent's distress. Empowering the child to believe s/he is better than a parent or others in the world also results in an unhealthy arrogance or grandiosity. John Bradshaw calls this toxic shame and it underlies all behavior motivated by the need to feel as good as or better than others. Toxic shame keeps a person incapacitated by and dependent upon the need for another's affirmation, approval or appreciation.

When a child is raged at or ignored because s/he has made a mistake, didn't follow an unspoken rule, or acted in self care, s/he retreats and gets cut off from the basic drive to evolve. This child will grow up stunted by the burden of guilt, feeling pressure to act perfectly, becoming overly aware of others' feelings and unaware of her own, or will not know how or will be unable to care for himself. Toxic guilt keeps us living according to what someone else wants, often in direct opposition to what would be good for us. Toxic guilt carries other uncomfortable feelings: resentment that we can never do it right, pain that our efforts to follow the rules are not appreciated or noticed, and fear that we will never be able to follow our own longings.

Toxic shame and guilt feel horrible and cause us to want to flee, hide our faces, or put others down. The feeling of self disgust can become so intense as to cause us to seek relief in suicidal thoughts or attempts. Some people can become homicidal to get relief from the perceived source of guilt.

Healthy shame and guilt, on the other hand, are more tolerable emotions and are characterized by a sense of chagrin mixed with a basic feeling of self value. Our minds accept that mistakes are normal and that we have a right to care for ourselves and grow. On some level, the mind also sees that we are the result of a loving miracle. We say to ourselves, "Oops! I'm imperfect. That's okay, I'll do better next time." We experience shame and guilt in the face, heart, and mid-back, by blushing, ringing in the ears, tunnel vision, trembling, or a feeling of wanting to disappear.

There are many variations of shame and guilt:

Accountability, responsibility, humility—that keep us honorable, highly functioning, and aware of our part in the greater plan.

Remorse, regret, chagrin, mild embarrassment—that reminds us that we are imperfect or that we must make amends.

Humiliation, dishonor, unworthiness, disgrace—that cause us to want to hide, flee or die.

Disgust, contempt, judging—that put us in a one-up position and out of our healthy sense of interconnection with others, tending to push others away or keep us isolated.

What goes wrong when we don't feel our shame or guilt:
We may:
-hurt others by our selfishness or narcissism
-lash out with anger to hurt, humiliate or
 disempower
-martyr ourselves and appear never wrong
-hold resentments
-offend others by breaking rules
-stay in limiting or unhealthy situations
-feel trapped and hopeless, powerless to act
-be unable to take care of ourselves
-get into legal trouble and go to jail
-believe we are worthless and vile
-be unable to ask for what we need or want
-be unable to eat in front of others
-become alcoholic or drug addicted
-be unable to know or tell the truth
-isolate ourselves
-lack a spiritual connection

What can go wrong physically when we don't express our shame or guilt:
-addiction related diseases (liver, lungs, brain, etc.)
-autoimmune disease
-debilitating illness requiring others to assist with
 dressing or toilet
-growths, loss of hair, distortions of the body or face
-overweight or extreme underweight
-sexually transmitted diseases

TOOLS FOR RECOVERING
AND PRACTICING SHAME AND GUILT

___ 1. Get clear about whose shame you feel. Whenever you feel overwhelmed or incapacitated by feeling less or better than others you are probably feeling the messages of shame you got from your childhood. Those messages came from adults or older siblings who were unable to manage their own feelings of inadequacy. These were untruths and now your task is to root out and eliminate them from your memory tapes. More importantly, they must be replaced with truthful messages, such as "you are wonderfully imperfect so you can evolve," "you are a precious jewel in the crown of life," "you deserve to be loved, nourished and honored, and your equality with others is a demonstration of divine love for all beings."

Children are impressionable and look to adults for truth and understanding. If you were repeatedly told you were worthless, stupid or never going to amount to much, you probably believed and incorporated these messages into your self concept and now struggle with little ability to esteem yourself. If you were ignored, left to care for yourself or younger siblings, or your basic needs were not met, you will have a difficult time treating yourself with attention, love and good care. If you were told you were better than the teachers, your mother or the next door neighbors, you will probably find it difficult or uncomfortable to "fit in," will alienate people by judging them, or will resist a partner's demand for equality in the power balance of relationship.

When you can identify how you were shamed and by whom, visualize yourself as a child and assure that child of his/her wonderfulness, brightness, and that s/he is infinitely lovable. Tell the child those people were wrong when they said or did those things and s/he doesn't have to believe them any more. Visualize their shame in your body; give it a shape and color, size and texture. Now, see yourself giving back the shame to each perpetrator. Imagine using a super-powered vacuum cleaner that can eradicate even the most tenacious shame particles. Suck up all the shame you can find and turn the hose toward the perpetrator. Now flip the magic switch on your vacuum and send all that shame back. See it landing on or around the offender. Notice what you feel. Repeat the procedure if you still feel their shame. If you hesitate to give it back, remember that the perpetrator needs his/her shame in order to stop offending.

____ 2. Replace destructive self shaming with loving self-talk. Probably the most effective treatment you can do for yourself in healing this emotion is to practice affirming yourself as often as you can. I cannot emphasize this enough. Change requires self discipline and commitment. Even if saying something positive about yourself is painful, do it anyway. Do it until you no longer feel discomfort. Do it until you begin to accept this new truth. This feels awkward at first, but you will soon find yourself indignant at the power and absurdity of those negative messages you were fed and which you have been perpetuating.

List the shame phrases you hear in your head in first,

second and third person form. For example, my shame phrases were about my intelligence and this is what I said to myself about myself:

-"I am really stupid."
-"Boy is she dumb!"
-"Why don't you just keep your mouth shut!"

After listing your shame words, go back and write an affirming phrase coinciding with your first list. Get help to write these.

My affirmations looked like this:

-"I am an intelligent, articulate, capable woman.
-"Valerie is really smart!"
-"You, Valerie, have a right to speak your heart and mind, no matter how imperfectly."

Now record the affirming phrases on a tape (cheers and clapping are a welcome addition from group members or friends) which you can listen to in your car, at home or work. Listen to this tape and practice along with it several times a day until you can honestly say each phrase with absolute conviction and comfort.

_____ 3. Accept that you are imperfect. This does not mean beat yourself up for mistakes you make. This means be gentle with yourself when you don't know enough or you don't succeed, no matter how hard you try. There are no perfect humans. What is perfect behavior? Perfect thinking? Perfect production? My observation of human beings has led me to believe that, as with nature, we are perpetually striving to evolve to higher functioning in all aspects of ourselves.

Given an accepting atmosphere, opportunity, and guidance, the human life moves through stages of development, gathering skills, experience and wisdom along the way. We are generally able to do what we push ourselves to do. Even in the final stages of life, people learn from mistakes, grow toward self acceptance, and find new levels of loving and being.

The single most important tool I found that signifi-
cantly changed my feelings about myself was the phrase
"I did the best I could." In most circumstances, given my
level of maturity and skill, this statement seems to be true
and lets me off the hook of self criticism. If, after much
soul searching, I determine that in fact I have not done the
best I can, I am forced to be accountable. This empowers
me to change my slothful or irresponsible behavior and to
reach for a more mature or disciplined (not rigid) way of
being. There is freedom in this. There are fewer mistakes
to clean up after and life moves more efficiently and
smoothly.

Practice the phrase "I did the best I could." Look back
at your life and list those circumstances of which you still
find yourself being critical. Focus specifically on your
part and notice your level of maturity and skill, and the
beliefs you held. Now go back to each aspect and say this
phrase to yourself. Be careful to not move into fantasy,
like "he wouldn't have walked away, if I had said it
differently." Stick to the facts. The fact was you didn't
know how to say it differently. You didn't know he would
walk away. He wasn't telling you what he wanted in order
to keep standing there. You might not have been willing to
do what he wanted. Accept that you did the best you could.

_____ 4. Be accountable. Shame can debilitate you so
that when you are wrong you struggle to admit it or you
accept far too much responsibility and make everything
your fault. Accept that you may have offended someone
even if that was not your intention. Do what you can to
change what you can and accept the parts of yourself you
can't change. Be truthful with yourself about your part in
what happens to you. Make amends when you offend or
hurt others, even if it was unintentional. Be fair in your
assessment and aware of your magical thinking. For

example you cannot wish someone into a behavior, nor are you the cause of another's emotional response. Be clear with yourself when you are acting with dark intentions and stop your destructive behavior. Use loving forgiveness as a measure for your behavior—for yourself and for others.

Healing words are essential. Practice the following statements:

-"I am sorry if I offended you. Please forgive me."

-"I am a little embarrassed. Can I make it up to you?"

-"I stuck my foot in my mouth."

-"I got carried away. I didn't think before I acted."

-"I was selfish. I was wrong."

____ 5. Practice honesty. Remember that toxic shame can cause you to feel like you are not enough. If you find yourself embellishing or understating stories, telling half truths, lying even when telling the truth would bring few consequences, you are most likely being driven by shame. Keeping too much change at the store, finding someone else's bracelet in your handbag, or not returning a borrowed item may bring temporary relief from feeling "not enough," but they add to the already festering shame core.

Lying and dishonesty can become so much a part of who you are that you forget or don't recognize what is truth. People will tend to disbelieve you after awhile or may resent you when you don't say truthfully what you think or feel. Deceit will bring more problems than will telling the truth. Be honest. Use honesty as a rule of thumb. If you are undecided, always go for the truth. You may suffer slightly in the short run, but you will live more freely in integrity.

What about if telling the truth will hurt someone? You must use good judgment here. You will know when privacy and discretion are indicated. You will also know what motivates you to tell or withhold. Keep self-serving to a minimum and trust people to handle the truth. Be honest with yourself when you answer the following:

- Am I being true to myself?
- Will telling this truth hurt or help another?
- Am I volunteering information to impress, hurt, or defile?
- Am I being fair?
- Am I telling the truth to the right person?

____ 6. Choose healthy options in the midst of overwhelming shame. As with other powerful emotions like anger and fear, curtailing shame and guilt before they become debilitating is most important. Anticipate when you might be vulnerable to shame or guilt and practice good self care. Eat well, get plenty of rest, dress your best in colors, fabric and style that fit your mood, exercise, practice affirmations, be ready with a list of optional ways to stay centered or get safe.

When you know you will see your mother on Sunday, spend Saturday taking care of yourself. If her typical behavior is to remind you of how you don't see her enough, prepare yourself. Affirm that three visits a month is as much as you see many of your friends and that you have a right to enjoy time away from her. If your father typically reminds you that being a florist isn't the "right" job for a son to do, spend time listing the things you like most about your work and practice telling him you appreciate his concern but you won't discuss your work with him. If you know you have to give a lecture on Tuesday spend the weekend boning up, organizing your thoughts and getting very clear about what you want to say. Then affirm your right to laugh at your mistakes.

Avoid abusive situations if you feel you cannot set limits with others. Getting abused verbally, emotionally, physically, sexually, spiritually or intellectually will only add to your unhealthy shame. Any relationship that requires you to be abused will not bring you the security, support or loving you seek. This kind of relationship will only bring heartache, resentment, loss of esteem, and more shame. Do some reading on love addiction to determine if you are drawn into an abusive relationship because you are powerless to stay away. These kinds of relationships may bring temporary relief from feeling like you don't matter, but they eventually will cause you much grief, despair and feelings of being powerless. Rules that suggest that you must get abused in order to keep someone loving you are skewed notions arising from abusive parents and do not serve you. Choose only supportive, wholesome, friendly and respectful relationships where you feel equal and honored. If your efforts to change the balance of power in an existing relationship do not produce these qualities, then you must cut loose and move on. When you believe you deserve more, you will get more.

____ 7. Get clear about what rules you are following. Guilt is designed to keep us accountable and cooperative. When guilt causes a loss of power, grief, fear, or stagnation, it is time to examine the underlying beliefs you hold in order to determine their current validity or absurdity.

Going to see your mother-in-law in the nursing home is a loving gesture and a demonstration of concern and loyalty. However, if seeing her brings you pain, verbal abuse, and disrespect because you didn't bring her ice cream, then you must change the above "rule" so you can operate more in your own best interest. Perhaps it could sound more like "going to see your mother-in-law in the nursing home is a loving gesture only of in going you feel safe, centered, and can set limits when she gets abusive." This frees you up to care for yourself, reduce the amount of visits, write more, hire someone to give her a massage, or send flowers instead of making a visit.

If the underlying rule or belief doesn't serve you in a loving supportive way, change the rule. In unhealthy relationships anything that looks like independent, self caring behavior will be a threat and will often bring cries of "selfish!"

or "disrespectful!" We need a certain amount of self centeredness in order to balance our needs with others' needs. We are not meant to sublimate our needs for another's all the time (even children). A friend can be a resource for feedback if you cannot determine for yourself what rule you want to operate within. Use moderation. Imagine life without debilitating guilt. You deserve this freedom.

____ 8. Demonstrate your equality with others. The need to be better than others arises out of the discomfort of believing your best is not enough. Arrogance and grandiosity keep you separated, even pristinely isolated. Shame begets more shame as you try to keep yourself apart by being different or better. When you do this you transfer to all around you the shame you are not acknowledging. You may demand perfection in others, blame, intellectualize, deny, martyr yourself, or rage, deflecting your own shame to others.

We transfer shame on all levels of society, even in how we treat our planet. We pollute and ravage, take from and use, indulge our greed and deny responsibility. Then we say "What a shame!" If we are going to heal ourselves and the earth, we must be meticulously conscious of the impact of what we do. Recycle, reduce consumption, conserve, give back in money or time.

Support homeless programs, intensive farming methods, and simple living. Teach your children respect for life. Volunteer for animal shelters, children's mental health programs, soup kitchens, tree planting projects, fund raising for the Sierra Club or Nature Conservancy. Demonstrate in palpable ways your equality with people, animals, plants, and the earth's water. Educate by modeling.

Managing your shame means being responsible for yourself and having consciousness of others and the earth. Find ways to practice loving regard for others. Notice how you are equal, even to the dirtiest bum on the street or the most elegant society lady. When the relationship with others gets in balance, we can begin to truly heal—as individuals, a culture, and planet.

_____ 9. Ask for feedback. Shame can prevent you from taking in both criticism and positive affirmation. When critical reflection is given in a caring way, the impact is penetrating and long lasting. This kind of difficult feedback can have the most beneficial effect in sensitizing you to another's feelings and needs. Ultimately, being able to receive criticism makes you easier to live with and a better community member. Also, receiving compliments helps you feel good and lets others know you have taken in their love.

Courage and strength are required to deliberately risk harsh criticism or rejection from others. However, the most effective way to overcome shame and fear of rejection is to ask for direct input. People generally love to give both critical and affirming observations. Keep in mind that you are far more harsh with yourself than most people would be in their feedback to you. Unhealthy parenting can sensitize you to hear only negative criticism and even to turn to negative the most positive reflection. You may have been told you were awful or were not even noticed. Healing shame requires the repeated practice of hearing compliments.

Ask a friend how s/he is seeing you. This can be about anything—your hair style, clothing, makeup, beard or mustache, your behavior at a party, a meal you prepared, how you handle money, if you are too loud or not assertive enough. Your feelings are not open for criticism, but you may need to know how your emotional behavior impacts others. Ask a boss for specifics about what you are doing well and what you could improve. Ask your partner what s/he has noticed since you have been practicing a new behavior. Ask your mother what concerns her about how you look or what kind of job you have. Even though you think you know everything about yourself, you may not know how you are being seen.

You can ask specifically for positive feedback ONLY. This gives others a chance to love you with their words. A simple "Thank you" lets in what is given and lets others know you have received their gift. When someone spontaneously offers you a compliment, ask them to repeat it and then tell them what you heard them say. This prevents your shame from deflecting away what you need so much to hear. Breathe while you hear a compliment and silently affirm your right to do something well and to be appreciated.

Finally, know that any feedback you are given is biased. Others bring to their loving, as well as to their criticism, their histories, preferences, jealousies, resentments and wounds. When you ask for feedback, protect yourself by imaging a shield of divine energy around you that will shelter you from ill intention and contain who you truly are, regardless of what others tell you about how you are perceived.

_____ 10. Spend time looking in the mirror. Start with five minutes and build to ten or fifteen minutes. Start with your face and move to your whole body. Wear clothes or be naked. Look without criticism. Just notice the shape of your eyes or mouth, the roundness of your hips, the curve of your muscles. Notice family traits, then notice your unique qualities. Turn and notice your profile, then your back. Move your hands, fingers, and feet. Look in your eyes and notice who is there. Smile at yourself. Remember the innocent eager child who dwells within. Talk gently to the reflection in the mirror. Promise to treat yourself with love and moderation, not with reproach and disgust. Practice saying "I love you" or "You are lovable and beautiful (handsome)." Build an armor of self love that is so strong you will be invulnerable to another's shaming of you. Temper it with enough humility to remind you of your equality with others as blessed beings on a splendid planet.

AFFIRMATIONS FOR EMBRACING
SHAME AND GUILT

Probably more than any other emotion, shame must be modified by healthy, esteeming affirmations. When you fill yourself with good self images and loving thoughts, there will be no room for the destructive; toxic shame will get rooted out. Be vigilant with these affirmations, for shame is crafty and insidious.

I am blessed with my imperfection.

I am worthy, I have value.

I deserve to be loved, honored, and cherished.

Making mistakes offers me the opportunity to grow.

I am a child of the Divine.

Through my imperfection I grow toward my best.

I am doing the best I can.

I embrace the love that reaches me through compliments.

I deserve to be affirmed.

I need not feel guilty when I act in self care.

I rejoice in my uniqueness.

I have a right to speak my mind or disagree.

Others see me as they have a need to see me. This has nothing to do with me.

I am not responsible for another's happiness or distress.

NOTES

(l) Mellody. Pia, *Facing Codependence*. NY: Harper Row Publisher, 1990 .

FURTHER READING

1. Alberti, Robert and Emmons, Michael. *Your Perfect Right*. Impact, 1970.

2. Brodsky, Archie and Peele, Stanton, *Love Addiction*. N.Y.; New American Library, 1975.

3. Fossum, Merle and Mason, Marilyn. *Facing Shame*. NY; W.W. Norton & Co., 1986. A family therapy approach to healing shame bound families.

4. Kaufman, G., *Shame*. Hazeldon Foundation, 1981. A basic reader on the nature of shame.

5. Mason, M. *Facing Family Shame*.

6. St. Augustine. *Sex and Love Addiction Anonymous*.

7. Ray, Sondra, *I Deserve Love*. Milbrae, Ca.; Les Femmes. 1976. A terrific resource for healing poor self esteem, as well as recovering from sexual trauma.

8. Wills-Brandon, Carla. *Is It Love or Is It Sex?* Deerfield Beach, Fla.; Health Communications, Inc. 1989. A look at sexual addiction, sexual abuse and it's impact on intimacy for couples.

LONELINESS

...And while the Boy was asleep, dreaming of the seaside, the little Rabbit lay among the old picture books in the corner behind the fowl house, and he felt very lonely. The sack had been left untied, and so by wriggling a bit he was able to get his head through the opening and look out. He was shivering a little, for he had always been used to sleeping in a proper bed, and by this time his coat had worn so thin and threadbare from hugging that it was no longer any protection to him.

...He thought of those long sunlit hours in the garden—how happy they were—and a great sadness came over him. He seemed to see them all pass before him, each more beautiful than the other, the fairy huts in the flower bed, the quiet evenings in the wood when he lay in the bracken and the little ants ran over his paws: the wonderful day when he first knew that he was real. He thought of the Skin Horse, so wise and gentle, and all that he had told him. Of what use was it to be loved and lose one's beauty and become real if it all ended like this? And a tear, a real tear, trickled down his little shabby velvet nose and fell to the ground. And then a strange thing happened. For where the tear had fallen a flower grew out of the ground, a mysterious flower, not at all like any that grew in the garden....

The Velveteen Rabbit
by Margery Williams

Chapter 11

LONELINESS

Loneliness involves the feelings of emptiness, sadness, pain or anxiety and is related to at least three kinds of isolation. Emotional isolation is experienced when there is a loss of an intimate relationship through death, divorce or separation. Social isolation results from a lack of a support system or network with friends, relatives or therapeutic providers. Spiritual isolation is the experience of despair related to separation from the source of spiritual fulfillment. Loneliness indicates a longing for connection with self or others and motivates us to reach out.

Occasional loneliness results from boredom or an extended period of being alone and lasts a short time. Circumstantial loneliness may involve a transition, such as a move, change of job, divorce or death of a loved one. This loneliness may last one to two years. Long term loneliness tends to last much longer and seems to be more about chronic fear, an isolated life-style, poor social skills, or an introverted personality.

Human beings thrive when there is intimacy, friendship and a feeling of belonging. Early on, children must experience bonding with a significant other, acceptance and nurturing, fulfillment of their basic needs, and training in social skills. Without such mastery, the individual is ill equipped to enter into significant relationships with trust, confidence and the ability to share him/herself.

When a child is mistreated, s/he will grow up expecting rejection, fearing connection, and mistrusting sincere regard. This individual will be unable to initiate or sustain close relationships, may even believe there is no need for others, and may feel misunderstood or unlovable. The isolated or lonely person is difficult to reach, may be preoccupied with acquisition or accomplishment, tends to be rigid or "walled off," and is often outwardly focused on others or things. Lonely people need time to slowly build bridges with others.

Loneliness must be distinguished from being alone. Aloneness is simply the comfortable experience of solitary activity and self reflection and is a desired state in the development of healthy loneliness. Healthy loneliness involves the ability to experience the pain of loss or aloneness while maintaining self esteem. Healthy lonely behavior includes the ability to identify a need for social skills, resources for learning those skills, and the courage to risk connecting with others.

We feel loneliness around the heart, solar plexus, and upper back. If loneliness is intense, we may cry, wail or moan.

The reason we want to reclaim and identify loneliness is to be able to satisfy the longing for connection, companionship and self acceptance that underlies this emotion.

There are several variations of loneliness:

Boredom, malaise—gnaw at or create acute discomfort.

Isolation, depression—alert us that something is wrong in the area of social or intimate relationships.

Anxiety, nervousness, agitation, fear, busyness—prevent us from reaching out, resulting in further isolation or despair.

Lust—can provide immediate, but short term relief.

What goes wrong when we don't feel our loneliness:
We may:
-get cranky, gruff or abrupt with others
-engage in frenzied activities or feel frantic
-lose or never develop a sense of humor
-create a life-style that keeps us isolated
  (traveling for a job, solitary hobbies, living in the
 wilderness)
-lack depth in our communication, stick to surface,
 petty or mundane subjects
-compare ourselves with others and feel less than
 or make ourselves better than
-monopolize conversations
-use relentless humor to keep people engaged
-compete intently in sports or work
-demean, criticize or ridicule others
-push people away in order to avoid rejection
-abuse alcohol and drugs or indulge other addictive
 behavior

What can go wrong physically when we don't express our loneliness:
-heart problems
-bowel obstruction, colon disease
-migraine headaches
-breast, uterine, ovarian cancer
-weak immune system, autoimmune disease
-autism, psychosis, schizophrenia
-exacerbation of any pre-existing disease

TOOLS FOR RECOVERING
AND PRACTICING LONELINESS

_____ 1. Get a clear picture of how much time you spend with others. When you are in the throws of an intense emotion, exaggeration and all-or-nothing thinking is tempting. Loneliness can feel like you are in the middle of a dark hole that has always been there or will go on forever. The fact that you had a good time visiting a close friend the day before may mean very little in the midst of loneliness.

Note on a calendar with whom and when you shared time in the last month. Notice what your calendar holds for the next month. Now identify for yourself what you think is an adequate amount of time or number of friends you think would create a sense of fullness for your social needs. If there is a difference here, you will tend to experience loneliness. Your tasks will be to create opportunities for more shared activities and to develop closeness with more friends.

Plan a party, join a club, take a class, sit on a board of directors, get involved politically, join a group, develop a new interest that takes you into the world, seize every opportunity to pursue a potential friendship. Volunteer your time in civic or environmental cleanups, attend a self-help workshop and invite a stranger to lunch. Join a team sport. Be active in manifesting what you imagine is a fulfilling social schedule.

If you feel the time and number of friends is adequate, your loneliness may indicate a lack in the quality of your interactions. Do you share your feelings and thoughts? Do you share honestly and with depth? Do you rely too much on humor or reporting? Do you use "I" to begin your sentences? Does the television serve as background noise to distract your attention from yourself or others? Are you able to hear and respond to another's pain, fear, anger or shame? Do you talk about yourself too much? Do you monopolize conversations with details and irrelevant information? Do you boast excessively or judge others? Are you open to other's ideas or opinions? If you are unable to assess this for yourself, ask for honest feedback from those closest to you.

Now assess the amount of time you spend with one significant person. If you have very little of this time, do you want more? What is preventing you from getting it? What would it take to have more? When you do have time, what is the quality of the interaction? Do you share intimate information with each other? Do you spend most of your time in conflict? Would you describe this as a time of friendship? When you part from this person, do you feel full or more needy? Do you both feel a need for the same amount of time with each other? Do you agree that there needs to be more intimacy and less activity? If you are not in agreement, what are you able or willing to do to get your needs met?

Use the calendar to schedule and plan weeks or months ahead. I have noticed that if a luncheon date is not in my appointment book it doesn't happen. Life can get too full of must do's. Keeping in touch on a regular, scheduled basis can keep friendships, even romantic partnerships, alive.

____ 2. Assess how much time you spend alone. Some of your loneliness may arise out of not having enough time in undisturbed solitary activity. Being alone gives you space to reflect on your life, feelings or dreams. You can do anything you want, when you want and you don't have to consider anyone else. This is when you notice that you really prefer to eat salad last, that you love to watch late night black and white movies, or that you sleep better diagonally across the bed.

Many people fill up their lives with people and activities in order to avoid being alone. They have confused aloneness with lonely. Some people believe that being alone is a sign that they are unwanted and feel shame. Others fear that if they grow to like being alone, they will never connect and will always be lonely. My experience is that spending time alone replenishes and refuels energy for attending to others and fills me with a sense of well being. I have more enthusiasm for connecting with my family or friends. Most importantly, being alone with myself gives me more to share about who I am and increases my ability to be truly intimate.

There are a myriad things to do alone, but just to give you a jump start: throw open the windows, turn on the stereo (put on Pavarotti), go outside in the sunshine, take off your shoes and walk in the grass, smell the flowers, watch the birds in the feeder, take a good book and sit under a tree, write in your journal, draw or paint a picture of how things feel, go to a movie or restaurant, explore a section of town, an art museum or bookstore, vacation down the Amazon River or to Kenya, take a music, art, or dance lesson, meditate or pray. Many new feelings will come to you as you explore life alone. Confidence and self esteem will increase. Fear and loneliness will dissipate. You will move from the oppression of loneliness to the freedom of being alone.

____ 3. Notice if your loneliness is specific to a person, place or familiar activity. A general feeling of malaise can take over if you are unclear about what is motivating the sense of loss. Missing is as much a part of change as is curiosity and anticipation. You miss the convenience of knowing the route to the bakery, dry cleaner and grocery and find it disturbing and scary to find the new route longer or more complicated. Your new boyfriend doesn't understand the humor or passion for rare orchids that was so much a part of the last relationship. Humans tend to hold onto what is familiar until something else becomes familiar.

____ 4. Let go of old relationships. Sometimes loneliness for yourself or a part of yourself will take the form of longing for a lost relationship. You may associate the fantasy of who that person was with the feeling of being full (probably because you were filled with your own loving when you were first together). You may also long for reconnection with a former lover because you long to reconnect with that part of yourself that was freely expressed in that relationship. Mental rumination on why you ever left that lover or how you could revive an unfinished affair is unproductive and misdirected. Focusing on filling yourself with and expressing love is far more healthy and fulfilling.

Refer to the chapters on Pain and Forgiveness.

____ 5. Counter your loneliness with productive activity. Loneliness may simply arise from laziness. It is easier to sit in front of the television or read a book than to call someone and risk being rejected for a date. Self pity may feel justified and satisfying, but will not feel as satisfying as a heartfelt talk with a good friend.

Procrastination can be another form of laziness. You have put off making that call for weeks. Go make it now. Don't wait until the last possible moment in the interest of "being more spontaneous" to accept or make an invitation. You will always have something "that has to be done" until you make connecting with others a priority.

Being moderately busy doing something you enjoy or get satisfaction from doing will alleviate some of the feeling of not mattering, stimulate creative expression, and give you joy about what you have created. Joy attracts people and diminishes the discomfort of loneliness.

____ 6. Develop a relationship with yourself. Find out who you are. Write in your journal. Write stories or poems. Write about something that is meaningful to you. Write about your likes or dislikes, preferences or aversions. Write your dreams, longings, most secret hopes. Write about your feelings, the progress you are making in managing them. Write an autobiography and include who was important, where you lived, favorite rooms or games you played, heroes you emulated, friends you loved. Writing gives you time and a creative outlet for expressing who you are.

Try new ways of expressing yourself in how you dress, wear your hair, use your hands, cook, or play. People around you may find it uncomfortable while you experiment, but you are doing this for you and they will adjust to the changes. My family had a tough time with my long skirts and funny wide sandals. I eventually outgrew this stage and they were relieved. I discovered, however, that I loved bright colors, flowing fabrics, and very comfortable shoes! Since I had previously worn my mother's earth toned hand-me-downs, this was important to creating my self concept.

_____ 7. Be a friend to yourself. Invite yourself to a special event and get dressed up. Buy a special gift you have wanted, have it wrapped in beautiful paper, and ceremoniously savor its unwrapping. Prepare a special meal, set the table with candles and soft music, eat slowly. Take yourself shopping for a day, just to browse and have lunch at a favorite corner stand. Use your favorite bubble bath or herbs and soak in a warm bath for as long as you want. Go to bed early with a good book, throw open the window and sleep in the moonlight. Have only loving thoughts about yourself, tell yourself supportive things, never criticize yourself unless it is done with respect and loving honesty. Only you know best what feels good and loving to you. You deserve a good friend like you!

_____ 8. Seek models and resources for good social skills. Your inability to engage in meaningful or even chatty conversation may have less to do with a defective personality than an omission in your socialization. If your parents never took you out or had people in, you were deprived of the opportunity to learn social behavior or etiquette. Your task is to educate yourself by observation and reading. (Movies are generally unrealistic and edited.) Practice the following:

-Watch people begin conversations or disengage from each other.

-Notice how people graciously handle preferences or dislikes.

-Start sentences with "I found it rather odd that..." or "Isn't it interesting that..." and especially "I am feeling...."

-Avoid comparing yourself with others, you have as much to share about who you are as anyone else. Notice instead how alike you are.

-Compliment others by noticing how creative or well dressed they are.

-Listen closely to what others say, maintain eye contact.

-Find ways to demonstrate or communicate how you value other people.

-Be considerate of other's feelings by asking what they feel or affirming how hard it must be to feel sad.

-Observe people with curiosity, rather than judgment or mistrust.

-Be friendly; open yourself to the possibility that someone will be curious about you. Talk to people. Smile and look at people.

-Use moderation in how you present to the world. People tend to be frightened of the unusual or strange. Give people a chance to approach you, and as you get more friendly there will be time to express yourself more creatively.

-Invite people to join you in a game or an event you enjoy doing. Don't concern yourself about who will like whom, just have fun and be curious. If you find you don't enjoy a person, let them know you appreciate their willingness to join you and be honest if you don't intend to see them again. Then ask someone else for the next time.

___ 9. Use the language of reaching out. When you are lonely let someone know. Don't expect others to guess what you are feeling or needing. And don't assume people are too busy to see you. Be clear with your requests for time and attention. Then give people room to decline or make their own choices about when they can be available. If someone is not available, call again. Getting your needs met can feel monumental, but persistence is the key. Keep in mind too that one of the best ways to get what you need is by giving it. Asking a friend to call you because you need attention may feel burdensome to him/her. But calling to see how s/he is may feel supportive. Your friend may be lonely, too, and unable to reach out. Try saying some of the following:

"I am a little lonely and was hoping you could talk."

"I was missing you, so I called."

"I am thinking about you and the fun we had last time we were together."

"I had a good time. When can we do it again?"

"When you think of it, I would appreciate a note or a call letting me know you are thinking of me."

"I would love to have you join me for dinner."

"When can I call to invite you again?"

____ 10. Give yourself the experience of being spiritual. Loneliness may indicate your heart's longing for connection with God or the world of spirit. Prayer and meditation are a direct and immediate route. Attending a religious ceremony brings the added energy and power of many people gathering together in a common focus—to bless, honor, praise, or heal. Losing a spiritual connection is painful, reclaiming that spiritual connection is joyous. As I have said earlier, finding spirituality takes time, practice and dedication. You may be fortunate to have cathartic moments of clarity and bliss. These are simply the windows through which you get glimpses of the divine that dwells within. When you have a relationship of faith, a conviction that you are graced with love, loneliness will be a fleeting reminder that you are far away from yourself. Then you will know to practice some of these suggestions.

AFFIRMATIONS FOR
EMBRACING LONELINESS

My loneliness is a gift to help me connect, not a punishment.
Through my loneliness I will find myself.
Loneliness is temporary and resolvable.
Other people are lonely too.
I am courageous in reaching out to others.
I love to be included by others, just as they love to be included by me.
I am really never alone, I have my self.
I have a right to need others in my life.
I have a right to spend time alone with myself.
I am less lonely as I share my love with others.

FURTHER RESOURCES

1. Chopich, Erika and Paul, Margaret, *Healing Your Aloneness*. San Francisco, Ca: Harper Collins Publishers, 1990. One of the best guides to healing the bottomless hole.

2. Goldberg, Natalie, *Writing Down the Bones*. Boston. MA: Shambhala. 1986. A wonderful resource for permission and direction to write.

3. Lee, John. *I Don't Want To Be Alone*. Deerfield Beach, Fla: Health Communications, Inc. 1989. Further discussions on love addiction.

LUST

...Now when the king's son learned that a grand princess, whom no one knew at all, had just arrived at the palace, he ran to receive her.

He offered her his hand as she alighted from the coach and led her into the ballroom, where all the company was assembled.

Then—a deep silence fell over the room, everyone stopped dancing, the violins stopped playing, all eyes turned to the great beauty of this mysterious one. Only a low murmur rippled over the gathering,

"Oh how beautiful she is!" The King himself, old as he was, could not take his eyes off her and whispered in a low voice to the Queen that it had been a long time since he had seen anyone so charming and beautiful. The ladies were busy studying her headdress and her gown in order to have some made just like them the next day. If only they could find stuffs as fine and workmanship as skillful!

The young prince conducted Cinderella to the seat of greatest honor and then led her out on the floor to dance. She danced with so much grace that people wondered at her more than ever. A most splendid feast was served, but the prince did not taste a mouthful, so intent was he at gazing at Cinderella....

Cinderella
by Marcia Brown

Chapter 12

LUST

Lust is the feeling of intense desire. Lust involves the longing for intimate, physical, or sexual contact with another person. Lust's purpose is to connect people for the procreation of the species and to motivate sexual release or pleasure. Two people are drawn together by the magnetism created out of feelings of safety and familiarity, curiosity and appreciation, and a physical yearning to merge. This feeling arises from the genitals, solar plexus, heart and can take the breath away.

Lust is different from love. Certainly, lust can be an expression of love. However, loving involves a great deal more than the urge to be sexual. Loving is defined by time, friendship, mutual interests, and interdependence. Emphasis is placed on this distinction because many people, especially young people, think lust means love. Men in particular in our culture are socialized to use lust as the primary indicator of loving and being loved. This makes for much confusion and a great many unplanned and unwanted children.

Unacknowledged or unexpressed lust can lead to "sexual anorexia" or the withholding of sexual feelings. Some women complain of having no interest or energy for sexual activity. This is often due to early sexual abuse and the resulting fear and shame. Observation also tells me that this is how many women create safety and distance in relationships requiring intimacy. In an ongoing relationship, a woman's lust arises from the feeling of closeness, safety, mutual respect and emotional communication. If she doesn't feel these things being reciprocated, she shuts down, withdraws and turns off. While males seemingly are more physically motivated to lust, their ability to be sexual without the preliminary "sharing" more likely comes from the need to connect in a very tangible and physical way. Men have a great need for human physical contact in order to get relief from their loneliness. One study showed that male babies are touched far less frequently than female babies before the age of two.

Prior to the new male psychology that is emerging, men were stopped by their homophobia from being physically close to other males. That left women to be the nurturers and source of physical fulfillment. Unfortunately, this has also created an overemphasis on the female body and its use as a sexual object. Pornography, the sexual abuse of children and relaxed sexual mores have created a culturally rampant sexual addiction. Men and women are victims and perpetrators in the shame based frenzy to feel connected and to get relief from feeling powerless and unloved. Lust becomes unhealthy when it is used to manipulate, self medicate or hurt others. There are several variations of lust:

Desire, yearning, longing, pining—get our attention and point us in the direction of connecting with another in a romantic or sexual way.

Magnetism and flirtation—the tools used to draw people together.

Passion, eroticism, fantasy—step up the sexual excitement and necessitate sexual release.

What goes wrong when we don't feel our lust:
We may:
-experience loneliness, isolation
-dissociate, lose touch with our bodies
-gain and hold weight
-develop eating disorders such as anorexia and
 bulemia
-inappropriately make sexual jokes and references
-retreat to religious fanaticism and moralizing
-judge others and their sexual behavior
-become sexually preoccupied or addicted
 (frequent masturbation, use of pornography, af-
fairs, voyeurism or exhibitionism, child molestation
or incest, rape)
-inappropriately grope, fondle, touch another
 without permission.
-have difficulty being intimate in relationships
-sexualize relationships

*What can go wrong physically when we don't express
our lust appropriately:*
-ovarian, cervical, breast, prostate cancer
-sexually transmitted diseases AIDS, herpes,
 gonorrhea, genital warts, syphilis, chlamydia)
-impotence, premature ejaculation
-hysterectomy
-endometriosis

TOOLS FOR RECOVERING
AND PRACTICING LUST

____ 1. Develop your sensuality. Just as you have been perfectly designed to have emotions, so too have you been designed to be sensual. The eyes, ears, nose, tongue and skin are the pleasure centers of the body. These senses enable you to experience the subtlest nuance of light, sound, taste, touch, or smell. Indeed, the human body is vulnerable to too loud, too bright or dark, too harsh or too malodorous. But what wondrous joys can be experienced through those little openings!

Use your eyes as windows opened to beauty. Begin to notice texture, shades of color, shapes or form, depth and shadow. Notice how light dances on skin or leaves. Follow the outline of a muscle or profile against the background of dark or light. Watch light move across a room as you sit across from someone. Look at both men and women. Notice the individual beauty of each person—skin tone or color, shape or size, hair color, hands, jaw line, eyes. Notice how people move or hold themselves, how they use their hands or toss their heads. As you take the time to appreciate what you see, you will develop subtle feelings in response. Now, notice your own body. Gaze in the mirror at yourself. Without being critical, notice all the parts of your body, in their imperfect uniqueness. That critical voice is the voice of a parent, jealous sibling, or clothing designer. Your own voice can be appreciative of the form you are given.

Listen to the subtlest sounds around you. Sit quietly, close your eyes, and take in the natural sounds—the birds, insects, or wind in the trees. Then notice the low murmur of voices, a child playing in the park, soft music in another room. Be careful to reduce the amount of noise "pollution" as much as you are able. When there is overstimulation by disturbing sounds, the body/brain will want to censor what it hears. Too loud, too harsh, too jarring sounds do not encourage sensitization. Rather, this is an exercise in tuning into pleasurable sound. There are many wonderful kinds of music that get the "juices flowing." Experiment with what makes you feel sexy or alive.

Taste and smell the wonderful subtleties of different foods. Fully experience an orange. Feel its roundness and skin texture, see its lovely color, smell it, and now taste its sweetness or tartness. Let the cool juice run down your chin, feel the stickiness as the juice dries. Savor the experience of the orange for a few moments before you go on to the next food. (One of my most sensual food experiences followed a ten day juice and water fast and involved three steamed green beans!) Eat slowly, chew each bite, notice what flavors you like separately and in combination or the different textures on your tongue. Notice when you feel satisfied, not full.

Your skin provides sensuous pleasure in both being touched and in touching. Touch is a basic human need—necessary for thriving. Experiment with touch by holding, feeling, caressing different objects with your eyes closed—rocks, moss, bark, cotton, wood, sea shells, fur, pine needles, rose petals, a pineapple, etc. Then concentrate on the experience of being touched. Notice how fabric, sunlight, cream or water feels on your skin. Get a massage or a salt rub. Ask someone who loves you to touch you often, caress you, hold your head, rub your feet, scratch your back, kiss your neck. Use touch in a non-sexual way to experience your sensuality. When it comes time to be sexual, you will know what feels good and what doesn't and sex will become much more pleasurable and fulfilling.

_____ 2. Take good care of yourself physically. Feeling healthy, lean and strong will get you closer to healthy lust. When there are layers of fat, weak muscles, or digestive problems, lust is likely to be the last thing in mind. Lazy physical care is easy in this culture; technology has eliminated the need to be physically active for survival by creating efficient machines, mass produced highly processed and irradiated foods, and created television, computers and electronic games which require little creativity. These things dull the senses and confuse consumption with pleasure. Healthy lust gets lost to laziness, untapped creativity, and addictions.

Good physical care also means honoring the body. Cleanliness, exercise, good food, and quiet living set the tone for feeling oneself. Too much of anything will create disharmony and numbness. How can you surrender to the sensuous physical experience of being sexual if you are hating your body, feeling too fat or weak or struggling with gas and constipation? Educate yourself to your own physical needs. Create a clear routine for your physical care and follow it. Write it down, don't tell anyone, just do it. Love your body.

____ 3. Open yourself to your sexuality. Many people grow up with very skewed thinking about sex. Some of this comes from the wounds of sexual abuse and some from poor education. If you have been wounded, find a good therapist who can work with you. Determine with your therapist your readiness for sexual activity. Keep in mind that being sexual is part of a larger picture which should include safety, curiosity, friendship and desire. Abuse victims must have a feeling of dominion over their own bodies—the ability to choose with whom and under what circumstances sex will take place. Being sexual with someone because they demand or "need" it does not give a sense of being in charge. You must decide for yourself when you want to be sexual.

Poor education is the easiest to heal. Most high schools, colleges and community health clinics have sex education classes. There are manuals and illustrated texts for understanding the sexual response cycle, genitalia and reproduction. There are crisis centers and university phone lines for prerecorded information on sexually transmitted diseases and other commonly asked sex questions. I refer many of my patients to the teen section of the library for resources since many of them are unsure about sexual values, as well as physiology, and are doing inner "teen" work. Asking a therapist for certain kinds of information can be helpful. Clients have been shocked and relieved when I have answered their question about orgasm, genital size and "normal" performance. The sexual myths adults have often originate in childhood fantasy, from sexually repressed or out of control parents or with equally uninformed peers. These myths can intimidate, frighten, and cause embarrassment. Healthy lust is hard to have under these circumstances.

When you feel ready to experience your sexuality, do some preliminary observation. Read a romance novel or see a movie with a steamy love scene. Notice how you feel. Then remember that real love scenes are rarely so easy or perfect. They are sometimes awkward and hilarious. Hope for the best and have a good time laughing if it doesn't turn out like the movies.

_____ 4. Use good judgment in choosing a sexual partner. The best way to determine who is a good sexual partner is to spend time getting to know someone. You must determine how much time that means, but I recommend at least several months. This gives you time to know a person's history, habits, and commitment. In this time you may also learn about a person's political, spiritual, sexual and economic values. If you decide that you have few shared interests after several weeks, you can exit without too much disturbance. However, leaving a relationship after you have been sexual can cause feelings of abandonment, betrayal, and disappointment. Many people stay rather than experience the discomfort of being truthful. Better to take the time to be careful of another's feelings by going slow, and experiencing friendship and companionship, first.

A critical issue for people these days is that of sexual diseases. Asking if a person is infected is awkward and uncomfortable. Telling someone you are infected is not any easier. However, the question is so critical it is a matter of life and death (AIDS). Be responsible. Inform your partners and protect yourself by asking. If you don't feel close enough to someone to discuss this problem, are you close enough to be sexual?

Sexual attraction can result from conscious choosing. You may notice how he rolls his shirt sleeve, or how she tosses her hair when she laughs, how he moves when he dances, or how lovingly she arranges a bouquet. You may also notice your body's response when he reaches near you for something, she stands next to you, or he touches your shoulder. This magnetism you feel will build as you allow yourself to be aware and not act on it. Just take your time in letting it build. You will both know when the time for sexual contact is right. This is your lust building. Enjoy the titillation!

___ 5. Have fun. Laughter is very sensual and can generate a lot of lust. Flirt, smile, look in each other's eyes, pat, tickle, growl, chase each other around (and be sure you get caught!). Write funny or seductive love notes. Being able to play and be lighthearted generates love and lustful magnetism. After all, lust doesn't have to be so serious. Isn't lust designed to give pleasure?

___ 6. Contain your lust appropriately. Be aware of another person's need for distance from physical or sexual touch. You will get nonverbal cues, if not direct verbal requests not to touch. To respect such a request is critical to avoid offending. If you are unclear, simply ask, "May I touch you?" or "I would like to make love with you, are you available?"

Lust becomes unhealthy and offensive to others when you have an affair (even if it is just in your mind) outside a committed relationship, when you are sexual with children or animals, and when you are sneaky, obsessed with or are compulsive about sex. Sexual references or being sexual in front of a child is inappropriate, as well. Healthy lust happens in the realm of consenting adults.

_____ 7. Occasionally practice nonorgasmic lovemaking. One of the biggest complaints women have is that they feel a lack of regard or concerned interest by their male partners. Men complain of boredom and a lack of variety in their lovemaking. Why not make love without all the emphasis on performance? Turn down the lights. Play some inspirational music in the background. Look at each other. Slowly undress. Watch the light move on skin as you change positions. Touch each other. Caress, kiss, fondle. Lie together. Turn and feel your backs together. Use the music to move around each other. Use your face to feel your partners skin. Go slow and lose yourself in the experience of touch. When you feel ready to stop, turn off the lights and music and hold each other in sleep. Remember to flirt the next day, or tell your partner how much you enjoyed the time together.

_____ 8. Give over to your lustful passion. When you feel an urge to kiss her, when you can't resist throwing your arms around him, when you simply can't contain your longing, act. Be sure that you have permission to grab and squeeze. or you may offend your partner. I have mediated enough quarrels and misunderstandings to know that a great many conflicts could be avoided if people were more willing to spontaneously express their passion for each other.

Make an effort to cultivate a healthy confidence in expressing your longing. If you don't, your hesitation will be misinterpreted as a lack of interest and you will feel frustrated and lonely. You may risk rejection, but spontaneous, heartfelt, lustful yearning is hard to resist. Take small steps like flowers or a love note, then a beaming smile of appreciation. Meet him at the door in something suggestive, tell her she is the most beautiful creature on earth, whisper in his ear at a dinner party what you would like to do with him later....

___ 9. Practice moderation in your lusting. Being sexually promiscuous is dangerous and ultimately unsatisfying. Limit your sexual behavior to one partner and ask that your partner honor this too. Without this kind of commitment you could contract a sexual disease and the lack of safety and trust will erode both partners' ability to be sexually open.

Feeling lust for more than one person is normal and to be expected. Human beings have preferences and appreciate beauty. Humans also "recognize" kindred souls and this can sometimes be interpreted as lust. However, feeling this requires no action or preoccupation. These thoughts should be kept private and not given much attention or energy. Lusting after another in front of your partner is rude and demeaning. Sexual or lustful loyalty seems to be a very important commitment in lasting relationships. Containing potentially addictive lust is necessary to the integrity of any relationship.

___ 10. Celebrate your lust! I enjoy thinking that lust is divinely inspired. The experience of orgasm is private and ecstatic, yet is the closest humans get to merging with another. I imagine the saints live in an even greater rapture linked directly to the source of divine Love. Lust may very well be a viable route to spiritual evolution. At least one can have fun trying to get there!

AFFIRMATIONS FOR EMBRACING LUST

Because lust can be so laden with guilt, the use of affirmations becomes very important to the tender journey to recover these precious feelings. Practice giving yourself permission to have and enjoy your sexual yearnings:

I embrace my lust as an expression of my sensuality.

Lust will bring me closer to another human being and offers me a way to express love.

I have the right to decide who touches me and when. I give others that right with me.

Feeling my lust is not necessarily a cue to act sexually.

I have a right to feel my sensuality.

I am sexually responsible when I inquire or inform about sexual diseases.

When I flirt, I am being playfully seductive.

I have a right to exit a relationship that doesn't feel sexually safe.

Being sexually aroused is part of being human. My task is to act appropriately by honoring other people's boundaries.

When I have an orgasm, I glimpse heaven.

FURTHER READING

1. Bass, Ellen and Davis, Laura, *Courage to Heal.* NY Harper Row Publishers, 1988. An important resource for healing trauma related sexual dysfunction.

2. Griffin, Susan, *Pornography and Silence*, San Francisco: Harper & Row Publishers, 1981. A shocking reminder of how sick our culture has become around lust and sex.

3. Lew, Mike, *Victims No Longer: Men Recovering From Incest.* NY: Nevraumont Publishers, 1988. A source of healing for male survivors.

4. Qualls-Corbett. Nancy, *The Sacred Prostitute.* Toronto: Inner City Books, 1988. A very important look at the various archetypal images at work in the evolving psyche; bridges masculine and feminine, spiritual and physical, in a Jungian model. Can be very helpful in changing how we view ourselves as sexual beings.

5. Ray, Sondra, *I Deserve Love*. Millbrae, Ca: Les Femmes. 1976. Includes important affirmations for healing sexual shame.

6. Scarf. Maggie, *Intimate Partners*.

7. Wills Brandon, Carla, *Is It Love or Is It Sex?* Deerfield Beach, Fla.: Health Communications, 1989. An important resource for assessing sexual addiction.

8. Wotitz, Janet, *Healing Your Sexual Self*. Deerfield Beach, Fla.: Health Communications, 1989.

JOY

...In a moment the palace was like a beehive in a garden. In one minute more they had found the princess fast asleep under a rosebush, to which the elfish little wind-puff had carried her, finishing its mischief by shaking a shower of red rose-leaves over her.

She was watched more closely after this, no doubt; yet it would be endless to relate all the odd incidents resulting from this peculiarity of the young princess.

But there never was a baby in a house, not to say a palace, that kept the household in such constant good humor, at least below-stairs. If you heard peals of laughter from unknown origin, you might be sure to find the servants playing ball with the little princess. She was the ball herself, and did not enjoy it the less for that. Away she went, flying from one to another, screeching with laughter. And the servants loved the ball itself even better than the game.

The Light Princess
by George MacDonald

Chapter 13

JOY

Joy is a state of pleasant exhilaration that enables us to be content when alone and may compel us to share with others. Joyfulness heals sadness and anger, loneliness and shame. We may feel gratified, carefree, or serene.

Joy can be expressed as playfulness, lighthearted teasing, generosity toward others, the creation of something beautiful, or irrepressible smiles and laughter. Joy is fun, feels good, and can be very contagious!

Joy arises out of many different kinds of experiences: feeling appreciated or valued, completing a difficult task, having a loving connection with another person, giving a gift, running, jumping or singing, playing, imbibing the beauty of a special place, a piece of art or a person, etc. Joy can be a quiet self-satisfying feeling or a more raucous feeling of unrestrained pleasure. Behind joy, love usually flows.

Too much joy looks to me like dissociation, denial, or a wall of pleasantness (to keep people connected but at a safe distance). While this kind of "joy" is more pleasant and comfortable than what it often covers, isolation and loneliness will eventually result. Some children growing up in explosive or unpredictable families learn that pleasantness is safe and doesn't bother anybody. Others grow up avoiding pain or shame so adamantly that being agreeable and "sunny" serves to keep the depression at bay and provides a semblance of connection with others. Whenever you get feedback that you are "always so pleasant" be alert to the possibility that you may be avoiding something uncomfortable. Some people can and do have optimistic personalities, however. They see the positive in most things and can turn an unpleasant situation into something light or even fun. We can all thank the powers that be for these human beings!

Children are the best models for unadulterated (literally) joy! Sadly, joy can get lost in the struggle to survive in the world. The adults I work with invariably express disappointment that joy seems so elusive and difficult to recapture. I gently remind people that the little child who knows all about joy is still inside, hiding and lost perhaps, but there nonetheless. If the child was told to stifle joy, the adult needs plenty of permission to have and express joy. Sometimes it is necessary to go to extremes in order to find a middle ground that is livable and acceptable. I recommend that people err on the side of too much joy for a while before censoring and adapting. If it is not permission you lack, but behavioral options, consult the child inside and ask what s/he would do!

Joy is generally experienced in the solar plexus, upper body and face. With joy comes the ability to breathe deeper and a feeling of openness or expansion. Waves of energy move up from the solar plexus through the jaw and contract the facial muscles into a grin or smile. Sometimes the body wants to dance, leap, spin or roll. There is a feeling of increased energy, vitality, and general well being.

There are many variations of joy:

Happiness, delight, elation, exhilaration, glee, cheer, excitement—compel us to jump, shout, clap our hands.

Frivolity, gaiety, playfulness, merriment, hilarity, goofiness—compel us to laugh and include others.

Bliss, ecstasy, rapture, euphoria, enchantment—compel us to connect with a power greater than ourselves.

Serenity, peace, solace—compel us to be quiet, reflective.

What goes wrong when we don't feel our joy:
We may
-feel listless or bored
-become numb, with no sense of comfort or discomfort
-despair, feel hopeless or become depressed
-rely on addictions to get high
-become spiritually starved
-be lonely (no one wants to be around a chronically
 unhappy person)
-feel resentful or jealous of others
-live through others, such as our joyful children
-get mean or angry
-persistently intellectualize about everything

*What can go wrong physically when we don't
express our joy:*
-heart problems (from the pain of not connecting)
-numbness in hands or face
-osteoporosis (from carrying life as a burden)
-bowel obstructions (from lack of creative energy)
-liver, lung, stomach, and blood diseases resulting
 from chemical addictions (drugs, alcohol,
 caffeine, nicotine, sugar)

TOOLS FOR RECOVERING
AND PRACTICING JOY

____ 1. Notice all the things you have to be joyful about. Are you or your family fairly healthy? Do you have companionship—a partner or a friend, children or grandchildren, a pet? Are your basic needs being met—a roof over your head, food on your table, ample clothing, a car, electricity, hot and cold water? Are you able to get medical and dental care? Are you even occasionally touched, made love to or caressed? Are your aesthetic needs met? Do you have a lovely garden, a special painting, good music, a favorite piece of furniture or clothing? Can you occasionally buy something for yourself or someone else? Are you loved, cherished, admired by one other person? Under the worst conditions there is surely something to be joyful about. The miracle of your existence is enough to be joyful about, everything else is extra special. Make a list of these things. Then sit quietly and reflect on the ultimate source of each gift. Notice your joy.

____ 2. Find every opportunity to smile or laugh. Bernie Siegel says "There are sound scientific reasons why we call robust, unrestrained laughter 'hearty.' It produces complete, relaxed action of the diaphragm, exercising the lungs, increasing the blood's oxygen level, and gently toning the entire cardiovascular system...Physiologists have found that muscle relaxation and anxiety cannot exist together, and the relaxation response after a good laugh has been measured as lasting as long as forty-five minutes." (1)

Read a funny book or see a zany movie, write a silly poem (and perform it for someone!) Read children's books. Go to a comedy club or make up your own routine, then find an audience. Watch the baby monkeys in the zoo, Pull off the highway to see the newborn foals romp in the pasture. Visit a playground and watch children play—they are quite funny characters. Norman Cousins writes in *Anatomy of an Illness* about the importance of laughter and joy in healing the body. Laughter releases endorphins into the blood stream, giving a greater sense of well being. At first, you may have to force yourself to laugh, it might feel awkward and uncomfortable. Keep at it. Laughter is like any other skill we have to learn, requiring time and practice. The rewards are infinite. So have a good time and heal yourself.

____ 3. Observe children. They squeal, giggle, jump up and

down, hold hands, wiggle, run and leap, pretend to be something or someone else, tell jokes that aren't funny and laugh uproariously, roll in the grass, and love to chase balloons. Practice some of these behaviors and reclaim some of your childlike qualities. Set your mind to discovering the pleasures of childhood by modeling after children. You may appear a bit silly, and you may discover that acting "grown up" is just plain boring.

_____ 4. Sing frequently. Singing opens the throat and heart centers where pain, disappointment or anger get stuck. Holding onto pain while singing is nearly as difficult as patting your head and rubbing your belly at the same time. Sing in the shower, as you work or play, in the car or on the bicycle, alone or in a group. Listen to different types of music, from different countries. Experiment with sound through your vocal chords; play with pitch or tempo, resonance or volume. Take singing lessons if you are uncomfortable or join a choir. Chant God's name in a church, temple or ashram. Sing popular music along with the radio. Create music with friends on favorite musical instruments. Have a percussion party! Then take dancing lessons—folk, classical ballet, jazz, or ballroom—to further express the joy you have discovered through sound.

_____ 5. Practice solitude. Learning to be comfortable with being alone brings much joy. This is especially difficult for people who surround themselves with others and do too many activities as a way of avoiding being alone. What you will discover after getting comfortable with spending time alone is that there is more connection with the inner self, less loneliness, and great pleasure in self discovery. (See Loneliness) Also, for those of you who are struggling with addictive behavior, solitude may initially trigger a relapse or cause panic (See Fear). Take solitude in small doses at first, building gradually to several hours a week. Soon you will find there just aren't enough hours in the day to be alone with yourself.

Solitary activities are unlimited. Emphasize those activities that will encourage quiet reflection—reading a spiritual book, writing in your journal, painting or drawing, gentle gardening, yoga, meditation or prayer, walking, stroking your pet, listening to classical or New Age music. Getting comfortable with being alone and focused on you opens you to a relationship with your inner world—fostering your spiritual awareness. (See Spiritual Pain)

____ 6. Find opportunities to nourish your soul. Spend time in nature, visit a national park (they are designated and protected because of their magnificence, uniqueness, and beauty), read an inspirational book, attend a ceremony, visit a holy place or sacred ground (this information is available in many books on sacred geography), go on a vision quest or pilgrimage, perform daily meditation or prayer. When the soul is sufficiently nourished, life will be far more acceptable, understandable, and inspirational.

We get into deep trouble when we ignore the need to go beyond the mundane; we forget who and what we really are. Life is an opportunity to evolve our souls through mastering the trials presented to us, not an endurance test. The miracle of our existence on this delicate living planet could only be the work of someone or something incredibly loving and joyful. Are we not the expression of this joy?

____ 7. Spiritual bliss is the ultimate experience of joy. Incorporate into your daily routine some spiritual activity. There are many options here. Meditation is a good place to start because often in the silence there is direction and discernment. I encourage people to explore various spiritual centers such as Christian churches, Jewish or Buddhist temples, Hindu ashrams, or a monastery. Prayer groups, ceremonial circles, 12 Step study groups, sweat lodges. satsang, mass or daily services are just a sampling of opportunities to explore one's inner life. Prayer, chanting, drumming, Sufi dancing, yoga, and singing in a choir provide the experience of grace in the body. Even if you are tentative about these practices, give yourself permission to explore other thinking in this area.

Many of us have been spiritually abused—frightened, controlled, and physically or sexually abused in the name of "God's will." (See Spiritual Pain) Human beings abuse out of a misguided or misdirected will. The experience of God is generally loving, supportive and in our best interest. It never involves defiling, wounding or shaming.

How will you know if you are experiencing spiritual joy? Said simply, you will know. Sometimes this connection in yourself brings tears of joy. Or you may have a pervasive sense of well being, an experience of compassion or platonic love, the desire to smile until the jaw hurts, or an inner calmness that you want to share with someone. Sometimes there is clarity, you see the overall "plan" or the interconnection of all beings. In this place, you understand the reason for pain, anger, fear, and shame. Then comes acceptance or forgiveness.

____ 8. Before you look to others as a source of joy, make sure you are able to generate and sustain happiness, contentment and spiritual fullness in yourself. Because of your inner child's need for unconditional love, which is sometimes felt in the initial stages of a relationship, reliance on another for joyfulness may occur. Romantic relationships turn the focus of attention to another and can leave little time for solitude and quiet reflection. As you require time away to be alone or with friends, you will discover a healthier connection to a romantic partner, a greater sense of well being when apart, and increased maturity when dealing with conflict. True joy sustains and fulfills us in whatever we do.

Use your senses to take in the world of sound, light, touch, smell and taste. Cultivate an appetite for experiencing the subtle information you process and rejoice in the pleasure of your human qualities.

___ 9. Spend emotionally intimate time with others. This means time spent sharing heartfelt thoughts, dreams, longings, needs, disappointments, failures or achievements and involves two skills—self disclosure and listening. (For to specific communication tools that can be used any time, see Anger.) There is joy in clean, clear, honest communication between people. Men have tended to be isolated and quite alone unless sharing with women. Women have tended to feel more understood by women. Men and women have tended to vie for power or position in their communication, loading their friendship with sexual nuance and mistrust. Poor communication may be keeping you from experiencing intimacy and therefore, from sharing joyful time with others. These are skills easily learned in a class on assertiveness, communication, or couples therapy. Contact the local adult school, church, mental health center, community college, or counseling center for such classes.

There are also many wonderful books on communication skills.

The most helpful tools for intimate communication I have found are:

- using **"I feel" statements** such as "I feel hurt, when you don't call" rather than "You hurt me when you didn't call"

- **making statements** rather than asking questions such as "I am thinking you don't call because you aren't interested" rather than "Why didn't you call?"

- **saying clearly what you need or want** such as "I would like you to call when you say you will" rather than "You never follow through on important things"

- **using "and" rather than "but"** such as "I love you and I am angry with you" rather than "I love you but I am angry with you"

- **including supportive statements** like "What you just said is that it is sometimes inconvenient to

stop working to call, and I want you to know I can
appreciate the bind this puts you in" or "Thank
you for sharing your feelings with me."
Employing courtesy and respectfulness in our language
generates feelings of safety intimacy. We can relax into the
joyfulness of connection with another human being and heal
resentments.

____ 10. Joy begets joy. The more you practice joyful acts,
the more joy you will generate around you. People naturally
attract to joyful people.

AFFIRMATIONS FOR EMBRACING JOY

Choose an affirmation to practice daily. When you feel
you have understood or accepted one, choose another. Remember, joy as any emotion comes in waves. As you master
each emotion, joy will naturally become a part of your
consciousness for it comes out of a feeling of being centered.
Repeat to yourself:

It is my right and pleasure to have and share joy.
I greet my joyfulness with lightheartedness.
I embrace my hopefulness as joy fills my life.
I notice my joy in this moment.
Joyfulness is part of my basic nature.
My joy is a reflection of God's love for me.
I am filled with joy as I notice the gifts in my life.
I am blessed with inner peace, serenity, and joy.
My joy transcends the trials of my life.
My joy nourishes the child in me.

NOTES

(l) Siegel, Bernie. *Love, Medicine, & Miracles*. Harper &
Row Publishers, New York, 1986. P.144.

FURTHER READING

1. Cousins, Norman. *Anatomy of an Illness*. W. W. Norton & Co, Inc, 1979.

2. LeShan, Lawrence L. *How to Meditate*. Little, Brown, Boston, 1974, Bantam, New York, 1975.

3. Lingerman, Hal, *The Healing Energies of Music*. Theosophical Publishing House, Wheaton, Ill, 1983.

4. Muktananda, Swami. *Play of Consciousness*. San Francisco, Ca.: Harper & Row Publishers, 1978. Muktananda teaches meditation with a thorough explanation of why and how. A very important book by a very evolved wise man, considered a saint by his devotees.

5. Siegel, Bernie. *Love, Medicine & Miracles*. Harper & Row Publishers, New York, 1986. One of the best discussions on healing oneself through love and self-care.

6. Tannen, Deborah, *You Just Don't Understand*. New York: Wm. Morrow & Co., 1990.

FORGIVENESS

...It was a miserable old woman who crept down to the lake that evening; she stood on the shore and called, "Little fish. Little fish." She did not think he would come but presently the water went bubble bubble bubble and up came the little fish.

"What do you want?"

"To say I'm sorry." The old woman wiped her eyes on the corner of her apron. "Forgive me for troubling you but I'm that sorry and ashamed— not sorry because of the cottage and the other beautiful things—sorry to have been so rude and so ungrateful. You're quite right, little fish. I'm a greedy grabbing old woman and I didn't know it. I don't know what got into me and that's the truth. I'm sorry and please forgive me, and thank you kindly, and good-bye, little fish." She curtsied and turned to go.

The little fish called, "Old Woman, Old woman, I'm glad," said the little fish. "I thought this was to be a sad story and it isn't at all. You are still the generous kind old woman I thought you. And now I shall make the cottage and furniture, your clothes and the maid, and the pony and cart or the car—which you like—come back and you shall have them for always.

But the old woman shook her head. "Thank you kindly little fish, but no. Malt and me, we're best in our vinegar bottle. We're used to it, you see. I missed my rocker and Malt missed his cushion, and I like to be busy and fend for myself.....

The Old Woman who lived in a Vinegar Bottle
by Rumer Godden

Chapter 14

FORGIVENESS

Forgiveness is the experience of relief or release that results from the removal of emotional obstacles from the path of love. When we are hurt, disappointed, shamed or frightened by another person's actions a natural response is to defend by cutting off loyalty, becoming invulnerable, and breaking the flow of love. Forgiveness involves a conscious decision to relinquish any expectations and free oneself from the burdens of resentment, withholding or indifference.

Forgiveness is best accomplished by a change in perspective. Time to sort through what happened, calm down and begin to reason helps in changing perspective. However, the fastest way to freedom from held pain is through compassion, understanding and respect. An unforgiving attitude keeps people stuck in the energy of misunderstanding, faulty interpretation and pain. Seeing our own or another's lack of caring or respect not as ill intention, but as immaturity or an inability to love leads us from indignation to compassion. Seeing a person's action or a series of circumstances as part of a greater plan designed to help us grow or evolve reduces the feeling of outrage and includes us in an act of love. Seeing ourselves as having acted in the best way we knew to act, with an unavoidable lack of maturity and emotional resources frees us from self blaming and opens the door to self acceptance. Viewing others as cohabitants of a living planet who are expressions of divine love elevates us above pettiness. From this perspective, life becomes a series of events leading us to higher and more refined levels of loving ourselves and those around us. From there forgiveness is easier accomplished.

Once there is a shift from old disappointments to conscious forgiveness, excitement and hopefulness for what lies ahead unfolds. Without this exhilaration, true forgiveness has not occurred. Instead, denial has more likely pushed out of awareness the pain or discomfort of a wound. Some people, in their quest for spiritual enlightenment find solace and relief in the fiats to "forgive and forget" and "turn the other cheek." I am convinced that true healing requires a process, as well as a decision, that involves acceptance and appropriate expression of the emotions connected to the wound. Saying "I forgive my mother" feels good, but may only bring temporary relief if the work of forgiveness is incomplete. With the palpable experience of freedom in forgiving comes gratitude, wholeness and joy. This results as much from the shift as from the awareness that one is in charge of carrying or unloading emotional burdens, such as resentment or shame. Suffering is not a prerequisite to joy, but only a motivation to seek the source of personal power or self determination.

Forgiveness is experienced in the solar plexus, heart area, mid-back, lungs and eyes. An expansion, opening, lightness of being occurs. We breathe easier, stand taller, and weep tears of gratitude and joy. A smile comes easier and there is increased energy and stamina. Forgiveness allows us to tap the resources that accompany joy, love, and spiritual pain/joy.

There are many variations of forgiveness:

Freedom, vindication, exoneration—indicate an unleashing of something stuck, held, or trapped.

Acceptance, exception, pardoning, release—suggest the act of giving to ourselves or others respect and value.

Hopefulness, joyfulness, exhilaration—follow true understanding and liberate the psyche to reenter the flow of divine love.

What goes wrong when we don't experience forgiveness:
We may
-lack gratitude
-feel life is a burden, feel joyless
-hold resentments, blame others
-mistrust, withhold trust
-be unable to have close relationships
-continue to be abused by denying pain
-not set limits with others
-isolate ourselves, shut down, withdraw from others
-act out in addictive behavior
-abuse others by punishing them
-feel powerless, out of control
-become depressed or despairing
-lack creativity
-be constantly disappointed because of our expectations of others
-see ourselves as wrong or bad
-find fault with ourselves or others
-deprive ourselves of fun, rights or privileges

What can go wrong physically when we don't express forgiveness:
-rounded shoulders
-back pain
-teeth grinding, tight jaw
-ulcers
-blood disease (resentment poisons the system)
-kidney disease
-colon, liver, gall bladder disease
-weight gain and retention
-loss of muscle control, multiple sclerosis, paralysis

TOOLS FOR PRACTICING FORGIVENESS

____ 1. Make a decision to forgive. Forgiveness involves the courage to accept both what you cannot change and what your responsibility has been. Answer the following:

-Are you willing to accept that you had a part in what went wrong (even if it was in not acting)?
-Are you willing to have a relationship based on something other than pain, anger, or resentment ?
-Are you willing to have no relationship if the alternative is one based on these things?
-On what do you want to base your relationship instead (even terminated relationships continue in our minds)?
-Are you willing to withdraw the expectations you had?
-Are you truly willing to get on with your life?
-If you are unable to decide to work on forgiving, why not?
-What do you need in order to decide to forgive?
-How long are you willing to wait?
-What part of what happened are you willing to forgive?

____ 2. Assess your perceived benefits and consequences for withholding forgiveness. People sometimes ride on resentment or retaliation for a sense of empowerment. Remember that you forgive for your benefit, not so much for the benefit of others. Resentment, anger and withholding hurt you by stopping the flow of love from divine source through you to another person. Write in your journal about the following:

-What do I get from this pain and anger?
-Where else can I get strength and power?
-How do I want to perceive myself?
-How do I want to see others?
-Who am I not forgiving?
-What was my part in what happened?
-How am I suffering now by not forgiving?
-What did I expect from myself or others?
-How do I want to feel about what happened?

____ 3. Be specific in your forgiveness work. There may be many aspects to any given situation which hurt you. You must consciously choose to forgive each part of your wound. If you lost someone to death, perhaps you were resentful or hurt by a number of things: s/he got sick, suffered so long, caused you to be the caregiver when you needed the attention too, left you before you could realize your dreams together, was drinking and caused the accident in which s/he was killed, left you with a huge debt or small children. Your forgiveness work must be thorough in order to avoid stacking (A current disappointment magnified by unresolved past hurt or anger).

Make a list of unresolved or unforgiven incidents in your life. Go back to childhood. Include events that involved your parents, siblings, peers, extended family, neighbors, babysitters, teachers, bosses, priests, nuns and ministers. Include organizations, governments, political leaders and their assassins. Include God. Now make another list of the things for which you have not forgiven yourself over the years and include things you did as a child for which you blame yourself. You probably haven't forgiven if when you think of a person or an incident, you still feel deep pain, shame or rage. You see that you have some work to do. Don't be overwhelmed. These things happened one step at a time, so must the healing happen one step at a time. Choose any one thing to work on first.

____ 4. Write, speak aloud or tell someone else what happened and what you feel. Complete your pain, anger, shame and fear work for each of the transgressions you listed. Then practice the following format:

Write a letter to or visualize your third grade teacher (for example).

Tell her **how** she hurt or embarrassed you.

Tell her **what your expectations were** of her and how she disappointed you.

Tell her **what you would have liked** her to have done instead.

Tell her **you are willing to release** her from those expectations (not necessarily that you accept or will forget what she did).

Tell her **what you believe were her intentions** behind her behavior (include her good intentions).

Tell her you know **she did the best she could** with her limited resources.

Tell her you **forgive her** and **relinquish her to divine love** where she can be healed.

Telling someone in person you forgive them can be potentially embarrassing to them, awkward or can set you up for a defensive reaction. Sometimes, however, speaking aloud your forgiveness can be healing, empowering and supportive. Timing and good judgment are critical factors. When in doubt, write it.

I saw Sam in a male therapy group where he worked for months on forgiving himself for his alcoholism and the pain he had caused his wife and kids over a sexual affair two years before. I asked him if he had ever asked his wife for forgiveness. Sam was surprised by my question and elated that he might not have to "eat dirt" forever. He went home and asked Carol if she would take the time to consider if she was ready to forgive him. They set a date for a few days later to discuss it further. In the meantime, Carol did some writing to clear her thoughts and feelings. She was able to sincerely and lovingly forgive Sam in writing and later, verbally. This couple consciously moved toward releasing each other from a painful and embarrassing memory. They had the added support of good communication tools, friendship, a supportive therapist and time. Choosing to love each other beyond the hurt and disappointment was a spiritual experience for both and demonstrated to each other their lovableness.

____ 6. Forgive yourself. Remember that you are probably much harder on yourself than anyone would be in any given situation. The root of feeling responsible for everything is in both the need to believe you are in charge of your life and the magical thinking of the primitive/child brain. You believed you were the cause of whatever happened because you didn't have perspective or experience. When some of you cried you got a bottle, and later you were shamed for your neediness. The belief that you caused mom's or dad's unhappiness was repeatedly suggested and now you struggle to know what is your responsibility.

Be kind to yourself. Own what you are sure is yours and let the rest be. Accept that your task is to make mistakes, change and grow, love yourself and others. Determine what lesson is meant for you and if you cannot see it ask a friend what s/he sees for you. In the interest of your health and the risks you must take to grow, decide how you will act in similar circumstances again. Say to yourself "I did the best I could, now I will forgive myself for not meeting mine or the expectations of others."

____ 7. Make forgiveness part of your daily life. Create a routine or a ritual for forgiving. Light a candle, say a prayer. Send love to yourself or another person (especially someone you dislike). Visualize the love flowing from you to the person you are forgiving. See love flowing from your adult self to your child self, from Higher self to ego self, from Divine Spirit to you. Close your ritual by saying:

"When I douse this light of understanding, I release to darkness all negative thoughts or withholding I have had about (Person or event).

I replace these negative thoughts with loving acceptance. About this person I will think (good or loving thoughts)." Then hold this positive, (self) affirming thought for the rest of the day.

Be sure to do this exercise with events that occur around living together, raising children, work, intimacy issues, or world events. Daily practice will cultivate a forgiving attitude and will draw people to you in love.

___ 8. Give yourself time to forgive. Avoid judging yourself because you are unable to forgive yet. Forgiveness follows recovering equilibrium. Sometimes grief, disappointment or shame require time and distance to heal. Letting go can happen in layers, especially with our deepest losses. With each layer, new emotions may arise. Just getting comfortable with the ache takes time.

Notice what you do to prolong your hurt, disappointment, rage or resentment. Do you fantasize or daydream about a former lover? Do you go over and over in your mind what happened or what you could have done? Do you call or write to complain or blame, beg or plead? Do you continue contact even if it is painful contact? Be responsible by not indulging in the wound through replaying or reenacting what happened. Educate yourself about love or romance addiction. Add some new activity or people to your life. Move on and get enough distance to grieve and begin your forgiveness work.

If you find that you are unable to forgive after a reasonable amount of time, go back and examine if you have fully expressed your feelings, especially anger. You will find empowerment through feeling righteously angry. Forgiving or excusing prematurely will circumvent the needed anger. Focus on yourself, know how you will handle things differently in the future, and then look at the other side of things.

Remember that hurt most often results from unmet expectations. I became very still and serene one day when I understood that no matter how well you think you know someone, no matter how trustworthy and loyal a person has been, a human being is unpredictable. The human mind and addictions can play such tricks as to push a person to the very edge of their beliefs and values, and beyond into the transgression of those beliefs and values. While this can be viewed as sad and reason to mistrust, it can also be viewed as freedom.

When you can detach from held expectations and beliefs about what "should" happen, then when disappointment occurs, it becomes much easier to stay in love, respect and commitment. There is strength in believing in yourself as the constant in your life. When you can do this, you find serenity.

____ 9. Fill your mind and heart with loving acceptance and project this into the community. Dr. Edith Stauffer suggests you start "good rumors" about people you are forgiving. By telling someone something kind about another person, you change the energy from tension and conflict to peace and harmony. You may need to alter your perspective to find loving thoughts about someone.

Mimi called asking for help in communicating with her supervisor, Janet. We talked for awhile and then I reflected back to her that she seemed unable to say anything kind about Janet. Mimi didn't respect her, felt Janet was intrusive and disrespectful of Mimi, and complained that Janet was controlling. I asked if there was anything kind she could say about Janet. Mimi could only find her breathing to be a virtue. I suggested she close her eyes, visualize Janet, float above her and out into space about two miles. From there, Mimi was able to see her boss as a child of God, co-habitant on the beautiful earth, and a human being doing the best she could. When she went to her supervision meeting the next day she worked to maintain that perspective and found she was able to forgive Janet her inabilities while asking for what she needed from Janet as her supervisor. Talking about this with me also alerted Mimi to how she had colluded with her co-workers to devalue Janet. She began to say kind things about her, told someone she appreciated a decision Janet had made, and refused to collaborate with any further "Janet bashing." The work atmosphere changed and Janet began to function more professionally!

____ 10. Practice seeing each person as a part of you. We

humans are connected spiritually, moving collectively toward a higher level of existence and functioning. Though we may fail, act irresponsibly, do something thoughtless or stupid, we generally do our very best with good intentions. Most humans, including ourselves and our loved ones, are incapable of being any more loving or mature than we are in any given moment. We are mirrors for each other so we can see ourselves reflected. When we are unforgiving of someone else, we may not have forgiven ourselves for a similar transgression. The values we hold most highly often come from decisions we have made following our own hurtfulness.

The Amish call each other Brother and Sister to show respect for other human beings. These words create an association that is personal and which honors the true nature of our relational existence.

We must act like loving siblings not only with each other, but with the animals and plants, rivers and land if we are to survive.

Siblings forgive more easily because they have loyalty to each other and commitment to a sense of "family." Cultivating brotherhood is essential to understanding forgiveness, for brotherhood gives us a reason to forgive—to stay connected in love.

"Forgiveness is the means by which we will remember. Through forgiveness the thinking of the world is reversed. The forgiven world becomes the gate to Heaven, because by its mercy we can at last forgive ourselves. Holding no one prisoner to guilt, we become free. Acknowledging (the Divine) in our brothers we recognize (the Divine) in ourselves. Forgetting all our misperceptions, and with nothing from the past to hold us back, we can remember God."

A Course in Miracles
Foundation for Inner Peace

AFFIRMATIONS FOR
EMBRACING FORGIVENESS

Affirming forgiveness is probably the most important of all the affirmations you practice. When you can consciously forgive another human being, you will find empowerment, joy and freedom. You will also reclaim your love. Practice the following or write your own:

I forgive myself in love.

I forgive others by releasing my expectations of them.

I embrace the freedom from resentment that forgiveness brings.

Generally, others do not intentionally hurt me.

My pain is part of a greater plan.

I forgive God (or my Higher Power) for disappointing me.

Forgiving another's transgression allows me to experience trust again.

Resentment keeps me bound in darkness, forgiveness propels me into the Light.

I accept and forgive

When I forgive others, I also forgive myself.

FURTHER READING

Stauffer, Edith R. *Unconditional Love and Forgiveness.* Diamond Springs, Ca.: Triangle Publishers. 1987.

CONCLUSION

...On and on you will hike.
And I know you'll hike far
and face up to your problems
whatever they are.
You'll get mixed up, of course,
as you already know.
You'll get mixed up with many strange birds as you go.
So be sure when you step.
Step with care and great tact
and remember that Life's
a Great Balancing Act.
Just never forget to be dexterous and deft.
And never mix up your right foot with your left.
And will you succeed?
Yes! You will indeed!
(98 and 3/4 percent guaranteed.)
Kid, you'll move mountains!
So . . .
be your name Buxbaum or Bixby or Bray
or Mordecai Ali Van Allen O'Shea,
you're off to Great Places.
Today is Your day!
Your mountain is waiting.
So...get on your way!

Oh the Places You'll Go!
by Dr. Seuss

CONCLUSION

In writing this book, I tried to practice what I was asking the reader to do. In many instances I succeeded. There were also times when I was unable to follow my own advice. I have had to come to terms with my resistance to practicing the suggestions and the reality that you, the reader, will have resistances, as well. I have said in many different ways what I believe are the most important tools for managing emotions. Hopefully, you will use what you can and strive to master what you cannot. At the very least, I hope I have supported you in being able to identify what is being felt in a given moment. My underlying belief is that if you know what you feel, then you have choices about how you will act or respond. And ultimately, you will have choices about how you manage your physical health.

Now that you have read through the ideas and suggestions, go back and really work to complete the tasks. When you have a great aversion to doing something, ask yourself why. If it is simply an old defense that you no longer want to have, then give yourself permission to try a new behavior. Take the risk necessary to propel yourself into a new life. If the resistance feels deeper, more intense, look to the possible origin and get support from a competent therapist. A therapist is not a judge or advisor, but a guide and compassionate mirror for the discovery of your own answers. If you don't feel safe in trying new behavior or feeling new feelings, then your focus must first be on finding safe people, creating safe circumstances, or looking to your Higher Power for protection.

Changing habits and old behaviors takes time and attention. My observation of this process is that when people are motivated, they will seek resources and work intensely for a period of time, followed by a period of assimilation and rest. I hope this handbook will be a resource for that periodic return to self help.

I have emphasized self care because so many of us know so little about what self care involves. Yet, I believe it is at the heart of what it takes to manage emotional extremes. You may have been led to believe that taking time to focus on yourself is bad. On the contrary, you are worth every moment you spend loving yourself! Focused caring for your body, mind, and soul will help you to know who you are, what you look like, and how others see you. When you care for yourself in a loving way, you learn what it takes to love others and what you need from others as they love you.

For many of my clients, self care is one of the most difficult tasks they face. Just remembering to look in the mirror, rest, eat or call for a doctor's appointment is a monumental struggle. I have suggested that a routine be created around grooming that includes quiet time, inner child attention, and spiritual focus. A headline on a daily To Do list can be Self Care. A therapy group or Twelve Step meeting can be a place where people help each other by asking: What have you done lately to love yourself? Nicely hand lettered cards or signs that are routinely changed are helpful reminders to stop and assess physical, emotional or spiritual needs.

Potential physical problems were mentioned as motivation for paying attention to emotional health. Over the years of adaptation and survival, people develop tolerance for pain, fear, disappointment, or resentment. Some people are able to withstand a certain amount of physical discomfort, such as chronic headaches, back pain or constipation. All this tolerance and adaptation coupled with addictive behavior, engenders numbness, loss of vitality, boredom, apathy and eventually an increase in physical discomfort or disease. The body hurts when it is time to seek balance and wholeness. Of course, there are degrees of imbalance, just as there are individual variations of constitutional vitality. The ability to tolerate pain or overindulge are not necessarily virtues. Ignoring the body's cry for help, invites serious disease and emotional havoc.

In my work of guiding people to emotional health, I have witnessed the "miraculous" disappearance of many physical problems. Sometimes the physical disease is too advanced and requires medical intervention. There may also be a genetic predisposition to a particular physical weakness. However, prevention of further physical dysfunction is an option for people willing to be focused and determined to heal. Healing requires self discipline, faith, manageable emotions and a deep conviction that health is the only option. Affirmations bathe the mind in positive, health lending ideas and provide a map for the body to follow.

You probably discovered in your reading and practice that each emotion is related to the others. When you manage anger, for instance, you must also be aware of the underlying disappointment and fear. Mastery of loneliness requires understanding your pain and shame. When you move toward forgiveness, so must you be able to embrace your loving and joyfulness. As you heal spiritual pain, the way is paved to heal the other emotions. When you practice recovering and healing any one emotion, you change skewed thinking, negative self talk and intolerance to change that underlie your other emotions.

Emotional stability is a balancing act that requires time, attention and focus. Time for self care, attention to spiritual practice and focus in community consciousness provide purpose and value, understanding and tolerance, vitality and energy reserves. With these qualities come assertiveness, righteous intent, and an empowering belief in oneself and others. These in turn, bring a sense of accomplishment and happiness. We are designed to function wholly, as evidenced by both the miracle of our physical organization and the hard won experience of serenity and faith.

I am convinced that the traumas children survive are not necessary to functional development or spiritual attainment. If anything these traumas slow us down and make the journey rough, convoluted and lonely. Invariably, however, the human spirit matures by virtue of its miraculous and undaunted resilience. Looking at why we struggle so, I have determined that spiritual evolution seems to be the goal, self discipline and focused intent the path, self love and respect for others the nourishment along the way. The struggle seems to involve peeling away the layers of misunderstanding to find the jewel of self love.

As you do your healing work, you join forces with many others who are actively doing theirs. Together we will evolve and demonstrate respect for the beauty and gifts of the earth. As balance occurs within, so will we create balance in community and globally. Only good can come of this.